UK
Circumnavigation

Ray and Margo Glaister

with very best wishes
& Happy Sailing
from Ray & Margo Glaister.

Adlard Coles Nautical
London

Published 2000 by Adlard Coles Nautical
an imprint of A & C Black (Publishers) Ltd
35 Bedford Row, London WC1R 4JH
www.adlardcoles.co.uk

Skipper's Cruising Guide Series: Copyright © Fred Barter 2000
Copyright Book 1 © Ray and Margo Glaister 2000

ISBN 0-7136-5355-8

A CIP catalogue record for this book is available
from the British Library.

Typeset in 10pt Palatino
Printed in England by
The Freeway Newdawn
Design & Print Company (London)

CONTENTS

CRUISING
ASSOCIATION

*During this cruise, extensive use
was made of the* Cruising Association
Handbook, *now in its eighth edition; an
invaluable source of information compiled by
CA members and based on their personal
experiences when cruising.*

For more information contact:
The General Secretary
CA House
1 Northey Street
Limehouse Basin
London E14 8BT
Tel: 020 7537 2828

INTRODUCTION

FOR THE LAST THREE YEARS we had cruised in the Baltic, reaching Moscow in 1997. A change was needed. I had also taken over as webmaster for the Cruising Association site, and needed to stay in home waters in order to update this through a GSM cellular phone and remain in contact by email. We had circumnavigated the UK in 1993, enjoyed the achievement and made many friends. We had visited Ireland in 1992, when we had vaguely hoped to explore its west coast but time and weather did not permit. What we had seen made us want to see more. What better than to combine the two, circumnavigating the UK and Ireland.

According to the *Irish Coast Pilot* (Admiralty Sailing Directions NP4O) gales are rare in Shannon and Valentia in June, the mean wind speed at 10 knots was at its annual lowest, and temperature near the annual warmest. Although becoming predominately westerly, southerly winds are more common than northerly (head) winds in June. June therefore seemed the best month. We would aim to round Mizen Head on the Irish west coast by mid-June.

We allowed ourselves not more than three months. To save time we would get crew for a fast passage around the south coast to Cork, cover familiar ground with a few stops to Bantry Bay, and then enjoy the scenery and meet the people at our leisure. We were not to know that 1998 would bring the worst summer in our cruising memory!

WARNING:

'Please be aware that commercial traffic has increased in the Harwich/Felixstowe area and extra care should be taken. There is a designated crossing area for small craft, both in the Harbour and in the Channel off Felixstowe. Harwich Harbour Authority would appreciate it if they can be used. HHA can supply a chart showing the suitable yacht tracks coupled with a local tide table. I think they are still free and if you want a copy ring Harwich (01255) 243000. There is now a high speed cat car ferry operating from Harwich to Hook twice a day. This has been blamed for causing rogue waves in the harbour/sea front area, plus the very large container ships that use Felixstowe have been shown to cause surges of about 2 feet around the same area. As you may remember, 2 feet can be the difference between afloat and aground!'
Eric Beaumont, Ipswich

'There are reports that the shingle banks shifted significantly in October's NE'ly blow. Fishing boats are now entering the river immediately to N of the shingle banks off Coast Guard cottages rather than using narrow channel close inshore as recommended in the 'River Guide'. Clearly extreme caution should be exercised until the river is next surveyed, probably in April 99.' **Tom Miller-Jones** 23/11/98

This email was fortuitious, as I was leaving the Ore the following day. However a local yachtsman had left early after LW the previous day and confirmed the old route is OK, and was unhappy trying the other exit without a transit. We left the mouth at 1100 (LW Harwich 0838) and had a minimum of 2 metres by keeping first midway between the (towering!) banks and shore, then keeping close to the shore (20m) until the depth increased to 4m. No problem but extreme caution exercised! **Ray Glaister.**

WOODBRIDGE

Tide Mill Marina is most attractive, popular with Dutch and Germans, and accessible HW±1 or so. Good showers, electricity, hoses. Diesel, near town centre with attractive shops and supermarket. First night charge £8.50 for 6m, plus £0.50 for each 0.5m over 6m. Dick Larkman's yard near the navigable limit of the Deben near Wilford Bridge specializes in laying up, offers very good value, and has two cranes to get up to six boats in or out on a tide. Easy walking distance from Woodbridge Station. Power points. Cradle rental.

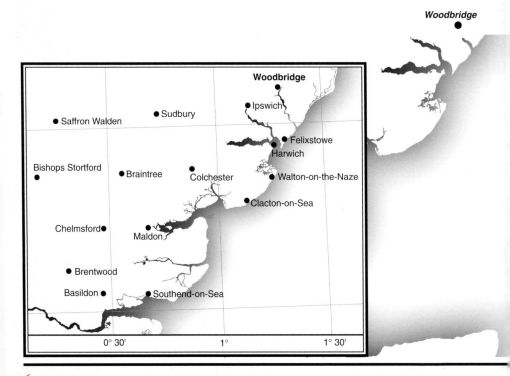

WOODBRIDGE

Friday 22 May

Disaster! Arrived at Tide Mill Marina to find the refrigerator temperature 22°C, and we are due to sail at 0900 tomorrow. Ian, friend of a friend of Geoff Doggett, who crewed for us last year arrived; he promptly made an excellent job of replacing the ring-pull in the cabin floor, especially necessary if we have to use the bilge for food storage at sea temperature.

Our daughter and family came for a goodbye tea. We called the Woodbridge refrigeration engineer who was in Frinton, but promised to come after dark. This he did although Margo and crew had already turned in. He found the leak with Fairy liquid and sealed it (hopefully) with melted plastic and regassed. Disaster dealt with!

BABAJI *at at the start of the cruise*

WOODBRIDGE TO BRIGHTON

Saturday 23 May and Sunday 24 May

(Charts 2052, 1183, 1828, 1892, 536, 1652). 120 NM, 24 hours 20 minutes

Our second crew Mike Perkins (Woodbridge Cruising Club) arrived, having just returned from the Channel Islands in his own boat. We crossed the Tide Mill sill at 0930 when the depth gauge reached 1.35m and didn't touch so were not too heavily loaded! We were glad to have Mike to pilot us over Deben Bar which we crossed at 1100. What a contrast to last year when we had the roughest sea here of our entire cruise to Russia; now with a light northerly wind the sea was smooth, but not enough to sail, so we motored out, soon crossing the well-buoyed and busy shipping lane into Felixstowe and Harwich. We passed close by Roughs Tower, a WW2 anti-aircraft gun fort on two huge cylindrical legs, and now home to an eccentric recluse. Crossing the Thames estuary is not straightforward, literally, as there are many sandbanks well covered at high water. With careful preplanning and setting waypoints on the GPS set, navigation is made easy allowing concentration on the shipping whose paths are crossed at right angles. The next hazards, after passing North Foreland, are the Goodwin Sands. We passed inshore of these through the Gull Stream, close past Dover and rounded the brilliantly lit Dungeness power station at midnight.

On short passages it is sensible to make use of the tides especially round head-lands like Dungeness where the tide flows strongly, but on this 24-hour passage we would have two tides, and in any case our starting time was dictated by the need to leave the Tide Mill at high water.

We managed a few hours sailing before losing the wind off Beachy Head, then short spells when the wind exceeded 10 knots, arriving at Brighton at 0945: distance on chart 120NM. Fuelled at 29p litre, and were offered day-stay at £5 or overnight at £17.50 less CA discount. The office offered use of their telephone socket and desk to send an email and update the CA website.

Woodbridge

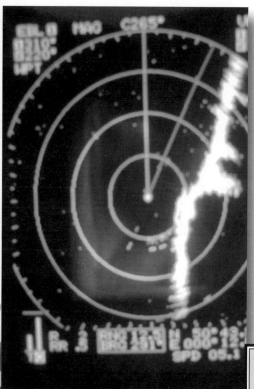

Overfalls off Beachy Head echos at bottom of inner ring

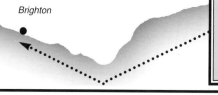

Brighton

BRIGHTON
New facilities include a health centre with swimming pool, 28 lane bowling alley, many new restaurants including floating Chinese, shuttle bus (£1 adults, children free) to Palace Pier, much new building. Resident boat owners moaning that their car park is being built on (a la Limehouse!). Entrance channel narrowed on ebb, but major dredging planned July. Now that everyone including vandals in Brighton has a key they plan swipe cards. Own web site planned shortly.

Newhaven
Visitors pontoon in Newhaven Marina dried at 1m - access and space less than anticipated from pilots but Marina restaurant recommended for enthusiastic if eccentric service! **John Langham Brown**

BRIGHTON TO BOSHAM

Monday 25 May

(Charts 1652, 2045, 3418). 40 NM, 8 hours 25 minutes

Up at 0330 and left Brighton Marina at 0400. We had been advised to keep to mid-channel in the marina entrance since it was low water and we only had about 2m in the entrance. Set sail and managed 3 hours sailing with 1-2kts from the northwest, but then motored to make the passage through The Looe Channel at slack water and enter Chichester Harbour on the flood. This passage of 2NM is marked by the Boulder and Street unlit buoys only 400 metres apart and about 2NM SSE of Selsey Bill, and saves some 6NM from the open sea passage around Owers. There are overfalls in the Western entrance hence our concern at approaching near slack water.

GRUMPY SKIPPER'S *private jetty*

The entrance to Chichester Harbour on this Bank holiday was like the M25 but without a central

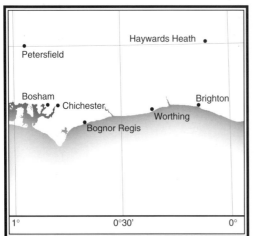

reservation, with all manner of craft at a wide range of speed. David Gestetner had offered GRUMPY SKIPPER's mooring off the end of his private jetty. We identified our welcoming party of Margo's sister and her husband but couldn't understand why they were not on the end of the jetty until close approach revealed it flooded and covered with a six inch carpet of slimy green weed! GRUMPY SKIPPER's huge buoy was likewise surrounded by a floating island of weed later estimated a 1 foot thick! By the time we'd inflated the dinghy and rowed to the jetty out welcoming party had cleared a path through the weed and led us to the Gestetner's French windows for a drinks party. Apparently the weed was the worst ever known and was blamed on hot weather and farm effluent. We were then taken in two cars to our friend's home in Bosham for lunch in their garden, followed by a walk back to the jetty and tea and cake for all on board. I cleared the weed from the buoy, using our dinghy to push it clear of the next mooring.

The Prices from the Royal Cruising Club had meanwhile returned in LECTRON to the adjacent mooring and I rowed over to meet them making frantic preparations for departure to the Azores the following Monday. I later checked our engine's cooling water strainer to find it apparently clear but it wouldn't reseat correctly. Turning the seacock, which would normally be like opening a fire hydrant, produced not a dribble, and much hooking out with stiff wire formed into a hook was necessary to remove the mass of weed. Eventually in desperation I inserted one of my warp-protecting polythene tubes, and with a mighty blow blew it clear. There was a gush of clear water at last!

BOSHAM

The entrance to Bosham Lake is just downstream of Itchenor, marked with a South cardinal post. Trot moorings line the channel all the way to the village. Most of the channel is fairly straight with Bosham's distinctive Saxon church dead ahead.

Towards Bosham a starboard branch of the creek contains many moorings whilst the channel ahead continues up to the main road. Bosham's quay is at the apex of these two with a tiny harbour approached between the quay and some old piles. To approach the quay, leave the South cardinal post to port. All of this area dries out at low water.

CHICHESTER

Approach: Beware that the ebb runs fast and in strong South winds can create dangerous breaking seas. The depth over the bar can vary according to the weather. At LWS there may only be 0.5m. There are good anchorages at East Head and Pilsey Island and there are six marinas. Within the harbour anchored yachts must hoist a black ball and an anchor light at night, and must not be left unattended for more than four hours.

Clearing weed from the mooring buoy.

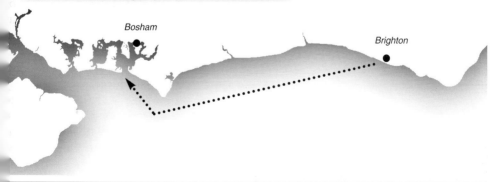

Bosham

Brighton

BOSHAM TO SWANAGE

Tuesday 26 May

(Charts 3418, 2045, 2615). 59 NM, 7 hours 5 minutes

We left Bosham 0900 after again clearing weed which had long trailers at water intake level. Today we had the channel to ourselves. What a contrast to yesterday when we couldn't see the beacons or buoys for other craft! After a smooth exit in heavy rain we made for the gap in the Horse Sand submerged barrier, then the NE Rye Middle buoy off Cowes, Hamstead Ledge, and Hurst Castle, and were spewed out of the Needles Channel on the ebb tide at 10kts over the ground. (The GPS set, which gives one's position, also gives the speed over the ground. Also called speed made good.)

The Needles

We had a good crossing to Swanage Bay, anchoring in one of the few sandy patches at the third attempt, only to have to move as a fishing vessel returned to an unlikely looking buoy too close for comfort. Most of the bottom is covered with kelp, which gives very poor holding with a CQR (plough) anchor.

could have used a Fisherman anchor, which holds well in kelp, but frequently comes up with a load of weed that has to be chiselled off with a boathook to make it light enough to recover. I prefer to find sand if I can, and having painted my CQR white I can see - in clear water - that it has dug in.

We admired the restoration work on the old pier, with a delightful shelter and elegant cast iron balustrades nearly complete. We'd been ashore to The Ship in '93 in life jackets. 'I see you are correctly dressed for The Ship,' the publican had said. 'It's quite rough out there tonight,' I responded. 'It's quite rough in here most nights,' he rejoined. Our crew went ashore to shop while I typed and Margo read. We changed our minds about staying, and after a fish and chip dinner ashore continued on to Brixham overnight, ending with a fresh NE wind.

nichester Bar beacon

SWANAGE HARBOUR

More moorings and seemingly more kelp on the bottom adding to difficulty in anchoring. Restoration of the pier, with delightful shelter and elegant cast iron balustrades is nearly complete. Lying in the south of Swanage Bay, the old harbour at Swanage gives good shelter from westerlies and south-wester-lies, although there is no actual harbour construction. Also to the east are the rocky outcrops of the Peveril Ledge, above and below the water, so visitors are advised to keep clear of the area unless using the slip by the lifeboat house. From sea the Wellington clock tower can be picked out behind the pier, and the area to head for is close in to the western side of the pier.

Moorings
Boats may be anchored anywhere in the bay away from the moorings, with sand and shingle beaches on which to land by dinghy. Some of the buoys are private moorings - but there are also some visitors' buoys available from the boat hire companies. Visitors are advised to pick up a mooring and land at the jetty or hail the Red Boats water taxi for availability. There may also be a deep water pontoon in the harbour for overnight stays and a floating jetty at the beach for which an hourly mooring charge is made.

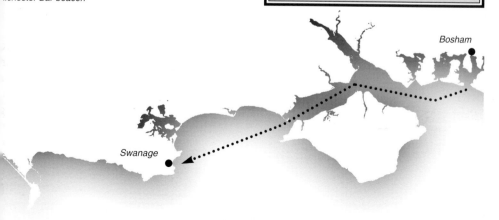

Bosham

Swanage

SWANAGE TO BRIXHAM

Wednesday 27 May

(Charts 2615,3315). 66 NM, 10 hours 10 minutes

We made an uneventful night passage, having first called Portland Coastguard to give them an ETA (estimated time of arrival) of 1200 at Brixham. We passed 3NM south of Portland Bill to give the overfalls a wide berth at 0200 (see opposite). Even so our GPS gave us a speed over the ground of 8.4 knots. Well out to see we passed a brightly-lit ship at anchor at 0300; it always takes a little time for it to sink in that a ship is stationary, especially when not in an anchorage marked on the chart. This may have been a deep draft tanker which anchors here to discharge part of its load into small tankers to reduce its draft and enable it to enter a port to complete discharge.

We berthed in the marina at 0900, three hours earlier than our forecast due to a fresh North wind, and announced our arrival to the Coastguard. The marina is built in the southwest corner of the harbour behind a floating wave screen, where it replaced the former swinging moorings, allowing many more yachts to be packed in. The overnight charge was £15.70, by far the highest on this trip, but those whose moorings were displaced get preferential rates.

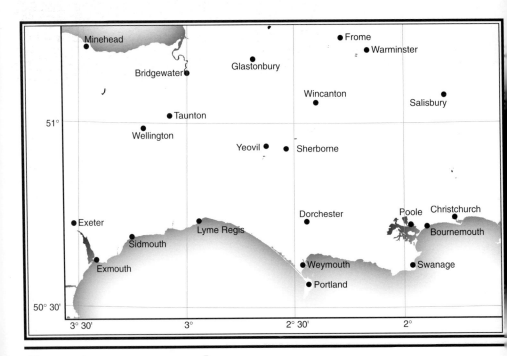

BRIXHAM MARINA

Brixham - MDL maintaining marina in excellent order. Their new manager started 19 March and was most enthusiastic, Brixham is still predominantly a working port with its main income from fishing, being second only to Newlyn in terms of the value of its catch. The Brixham fishing fleet has grown steadily over the last two decades and there are now some 140 vessels based in the harbour. Brixham is also an important pilotage station for shipping, with the embarking and landing of Channel Pilots. In addition, Brixham is a popular yachting venue and there are a large number ot yacht moorings and many pleasure boats operating from the harbour during the season. The Victoria Breakwater, which shelters the outer harbour, was completed in 1916 and is 3/4 mile long. The white lighthouse on the outer end (0cc. Red 15 sec) was only electrified in1980. Until then it was one of the last lighthouses in the country to be oil lit and mechanically wound daily.

Approach

Brixham is at the southern end of Tor Bay just west ot Berry Head. The seaward approaches trom any direction present no obstructions or ditficulty at all. In fact the entrance to the outer harbour can be made in any state of tide or weather conditions. Once past the port and starboard channel marker buoys stay in the fairway unless anchoring, and proceed to the marina entrance which is between the marina wave screen to port and the fish quay wall to starboard. By night this heading is marked by a sectored isophase light every 5 secs, vis 6 miles. Stay in the white sector and turn to port when past the wave screen (between vertical

pairs ot fixed and flashing red lights).
The Harbour Office is by the New Fish Quay. This is the main office for the management of the Torbay harbours.

Marina

Brixham Marina is comparatively new and so has all the facilities associated with such a modern development. The pontoons are well lit with power/water pedestals every few berths. There is very good security, with access to the pontoons gained only through a key coded locked door actually in the office block at the pierhead, so it is impossible to gain access to, or leave the pontoons without being seen by the 24 hour security officer. A separate toilet/shower block has laundrette facilities and the old harbour and town are only half a mile away.

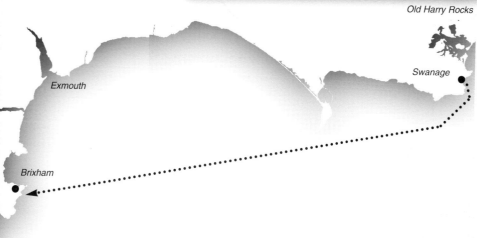

Old Harry Rocks

Swanage

Exmouth

Brixham

BRIXHAM TO SALCOMBE

Thursday 28 May

(Charts 1613, 28). 21 NM, 5 hours 45 minutes

We were now a day ahead of schedule for a crew change, and so stopped at Salcombe which did not seem to have changed since my last visit many years ago, although I suspect the buoys at £1.05 per metre have gone up! We had to share a buoy; it must be terribly crowded in season. A really lovely place.

Strangely this passage was the first I ever made, and as crew on an engineless Folkboat. After a breakfast from the ship's stores of sardines, chocolate and black coffee I had been seasick for the first time. 'No need to bring any food,' I'd been told, 'my ship is well victualled'. I have since contemplated repeating this mixture to check its effect on terra firma! A kettle kept filled was the sole fire extinguisher, but was boiling when the skipper set fire to his knees with burning methylated spirits while trying to light a Tilley lamp; he did not appreciate the idea of replacing burns with scalds! We had taken some hours tacking into Salcombe against the ebb. After this stuck with dinghy sailing for many years!

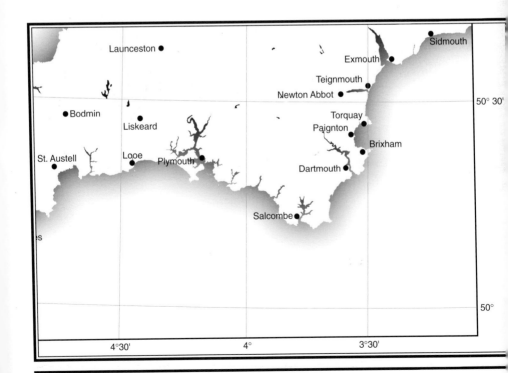

SALCOMBE MARINA

Salcombe lies in the shelter of Prawle Point and Bolt Head. The most southerly harbour on the Devon coast it enjoys the benefits of the Gulf Stream and a gentle climate which adds to its popularity as the venue for a variety of summer sailing regattas. The whole harbour complex inside the bar is in fact not an estuary as it is commonly misnamed, for it has no major river running into it, but instead is a 'na', a series of flooded valleys spread out like a hand with splayed fingers pushing into the hilly topography of South Devon. In part this accounts for the wonderfully clean beaches on both sides of the harbour at South Sands and Portlemouth. As little fresh water enters the 'na', salt water can be found up to 5 miles from the coast providing ideal conditions for many forms of marine life including corals, saltwater anemones and fish of all sorts. For many decades the waters off Salcombe have proved an excellent hunting ground for specimen fish and sometimes the exotic visitor such as the Gilt Head Bream or the Long Finned Tunny.

The town itself is compact and easily explored. The narrow streets tumble down the steep hills to the waterside where the main street, Fore Street, runs parallel to the harbour. Everywhere there are small shops selling everything from tourist souvenirs to hand painted portraits of your favourite pet, and from dinner plate sized pasties to freshly caught crab. The town is liberally supplied with pubs and bars and has restaurants to cater for every taste. You really need to spend more than one night here just to enjoy to the full the 'party atmosphere' ashore.

Approach: There is a sand bar which will cause heavy seas in any south to southeast winds or swell on the ebb. It is best to aim for entrance at or near HW. There are berths alongside the pontoons and plenty of anchorages. A very pretty and safe location with many facilities.

Brixham Harbour

Brixham

Salcombe

Friday 29 May

(Charts 1613, 30).
15 NM, 4 hours 25 minutes

BABAJI with Mike, Ian and Margo

Our log, a little paddle-wheel on the bottom of our hull that measures our distance and speed through the water, sometimes becomes fouled on thin strands of seaweed. This is not noticed until one starts, as this morning, and the boat speed remains stubbornly at zero. The log is on a plunger that can be removed, producing a fire hydrant jet of water into the bilge; something I avoid doing under way. It can often be cleared by rotating it through 180° which unwinds the seaweed. This morning this failed but later mysteriously cleared itself. If seriously dependent for navigation on distance through the water I deploy a Walker towed log, but this is a hazard in itself, having been known to be bitten clean off (by a shark?) and on one occasion get wrapped around the propeller after going astern to drive the anchor home.

Arriving at Plymouth we made VHF calls to Queen Anne's Battery, Mayflower and Sutton marinas, and found they were all full. Fortunately the new Plymouth Yacht Haven had plenty of space and will be very nice when finished. It had spaces for 200 boats on pontoons, and a fine new amenities block was also under construction. It will probably be good for the established marinas to have some new and healthy competition. The Cruising Association's HLR (Honorary Local Representative) E Cartner found us quite by chance, and gave us great welcome!

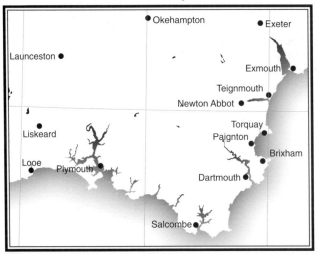

PLYMOUTH

If approaching Plymouth for the first time yachtsmen should be aware of the Firing Range at Wembury, HMS Cambridge. When firing is in progress large red flags are flown from Wembury Point and Penlee Point. The range monitors VHF Ch 16, working on Ch 11, call sign 'Wembury Range' to report your movements or Tel: 01752 862779 or freephone 0800 833608 for further information. When firing is in progress it is best to avoid this area if possible and pass to the west side of the Eddystone Lighthouse.

Plymouth Sound can be entered by either the Western or Eastern Channels, both of which are well marked. Tinker Shoal south of the breakwater is buoyed and should be avoided in southerly winds when the sea breaks heavily over it. No mooring or landing is permitted on the breakwater. Once inside the Sound the deep water channels are clearly marked. These are best avoided as they are heavily used by naval ships, cross channel ferries, freighters and the Plymouth fishing fleet. When practicable, cross the channels at right angles.

QUEEN ANNE'S BATTERY

A modern marina with 260 berths and a visitors' basin protected by a substantial breakwater and double wave screen. QAB is situated at the northeastern corner of Plymouth Sound . All berths have access to power and water and can be accessed at any state of the tide. The marina reception office can be contacted on VHF Channels 37 and 80 and is open 24 hrs, 7 days a week.

MAYFLOWER INTERNATIONAL MARINA

This is a safe deep water harbour situated at the mouth of the River Tamar.The marina is safely accessible at all states of the tide, has power to all berths, excellent new toilet, shower and bath facilities, a launderette and a wonderful bar and restaurant. In the summer months there is a courtesy coach to town for those who do not relish the 15 minute walk. Call on VHF Ch 80 or 37, a listening watch is kept 24 hours. Tel. 01752 556633/567106.

SUTTON HARBOUR MARINA

In the northeastern corner of Plymouth Sound adjacent to the eastern part of the City of Plymouth itself. To approach the entrance pass through Cobbler's channel and then turn to port in front of the Royal Citadel leaving Queen Anne's Battery marina on your starboard side. Entrance is via a 44 metre x 12 metre lock giving free, round the clock access, at any state of the tide. The lock keeper keeps a listening watch on VHF Channel 12 and scans 16, 37 and 80. Tel: harbour office 01752 664186.

ymouth Yacht Haven

Plymouth

Salcombe

19

PLYMOUTH TO ST MAWES

Saturday 30 May

(Chart 1267).
7 hours 50 minutes

My replacement crew, Dick Blamey, arrived at 1000 with his wife and mother to inspect BABAJI; they appeared well satisfied with his berth and left him with us. We left Plymouth at 1120 and made a good 6 knots under double-reefed mizzen and half-reefed genoa in a NE F6-7 and prolonged gusts of 40 knots, towards the Lizard. The sea became very rough, and due to our late start we were not going to round the Lizard before the tide turned both against us and the wind. At th rate we would not arrive before daybreak, so we gybed NW and entered St Maw giving blissful shelter.

On the way to St Mawes

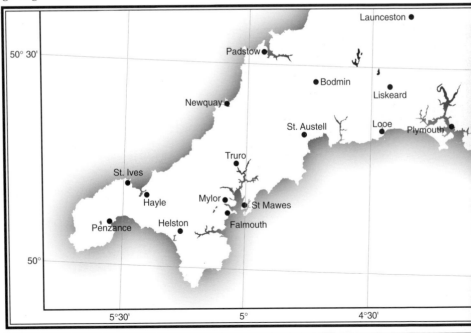

The schooner PHOENIX was anchored in St Mawes, taking us back a century or so! The forecast at 2018 on Navtex was a little better so we planned to listen to the shipping forecast at 0535. The first Navtex forecast is at 0848 and is a repeat of the 0535 forecast. We had a delightfully sheltered anchorage with a theatrical backdrop of illuminated house windows seeming very close after dark. Our son's email dated 30 May read "Hope that it's warmer when you get to the Scillies than it was when we went past - it was only 12°C and very rough - no fun at all!" This from a minesweeper!

PHOENIX at St Mawes

ST MAWES

This is one of the many fine harbours to visit when in the Falmouth River. Remember that the channel to Percuil is complicated, unmarked and with many oyster beds and moorings on both banks. St Mawes has a deep entrance to the anchorage in front of the town which is exposed in SW winds. Keep St Mawes cardinal mark to port. There is a small quay for landing but it is busy and used by ferries. Further into the Percuil River you have Place Manor at the head of a small creek and more sheltered private moorings beyond Amsterdam Point. On the left is Freshwater Boatyard and further up river (somewhat tidal) is Percuil Sailing Club and Percuil Boatyard.

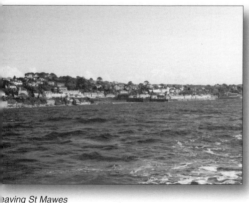

Leaving St Mawes

Plymouth

St Mawes

Sunday 31 May

15 NM

The 0535 forecast was in fact no better, so after a lie in bed we put into Falmouth Town Marina for diesel, water and provisions. We picked up a vacant mooring off Mylor, once a quiet anchorage and now crowded with moorings. We watched Dart 18s racing at great speed. Rather than return to St Mawes we decided to stay overnight in that south coast gem, the Helford River. Leaving the harbour for

Moorings off Mylor

Helford showed how rough the sea still was. Tranquillity reigned once again as we entered the well-sheltered Helford River where we picked up a visitors' mooring

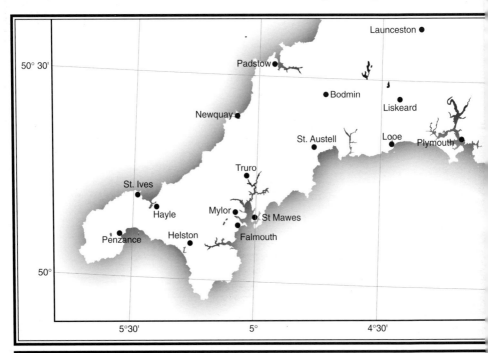

Use of a private pontoon for tenders, with a well made path to the road, is charged at £1 payable to an honesty box, a very efficient means of collection. Close by the most attractive Shipwrights Inn has palm trees and outside tables overlooking the creek. The Inn and surroundings hadn't changed since our last visit many years ago; the beer and food are still good. The chef uses an outdoor BBQ so you see what's cooking on arrival.

FALMOUTH

Mylor Creek

Now has hundreds of private moorings and anchoring would be difficult.

Helford

Private pontoon for dinghies is good value at £1. Shipwrights Inn serving excellent food and draught beer. Hardly changed in years. No Vodafone signal at the Inn or on moorings.The Fal Estuary and its associated creeks form the third largest natural harbour in the world.

The harbour was formed during the ice age when rising sea levels drowned the river valleys, forming the deep winding channels which lead some eight miles inland from Falmouth itself all the way to Truro, the County town of Cornwall. The area known as Carrick Roads stetches from Black Rock at the entrance of the harbour to Trelissick Woods and covers four square miles of sheltered inland sailing waters. There are five main anchorages for yachtsmen within the harbour, Falmouth Town itself, Penryn River, Mylor, St Mawes and Truro.

Approaches

Entry to the harbour is safe at all states of the tide, with deep water for yachts. St Anthony lighthouse guards the eastern side of the entrance. There is a drying rock in the entrance, Black Rock, clearly marked by a large beacon and buoy to the east, and yachts may pass on either side. Turning to starboard will take you into St Mawes harbour, and northwards into the main body of Carrick Roads leads to Mylor, St Just, the River Fal, Truro and Malpas. Bearing west past Falmouth docks leads to Falmouth Town and the Penryn River. Beware of large commercial shipping movements in the docks. Falmouth Harbour Commissioners administer the inner harbour and have a limited number of visitors', moorings, and a Yacht Haven with floating pontoon, fuel and showers. Call "Falmouth Harbour Radio" on VHF Ch16/12,Tel:01326312285.

Returning to Carrick Roads the harbour stretches four miles north and one mile wide. It is deep enough for sailing craft everywhere except off Penarrow Point at LWS. On the eastern shore is St Just creek with its ancient church and Pascoes Boatyard. On the western side of the Roads is Mylor Yacht Harbour. The harbour, set amidst unspoilt countryside, is situated in a sheltered bay at the mouth of Mylor Creek. Mylor Yacht Harbour itself is comprehensively equipped for all yachtsman's needs, and is accessible at all states of the tide.

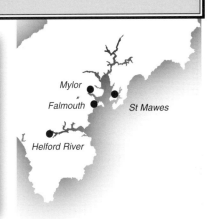

Mylor

Falmouth

St Mawes

Helford River

Tranquility in Helford

HELFORD RIVER TO ST MARY'S (Isles of Scilly)

Monday 1 June

(Charts 777, 1148, 34).
61NM, 11 hours 35 minutes

The 0535 forecast was much better, so we left at 0710 with a 16 knots SSE wind. Rocks extend for a mile off Manacle Point, but are safely cleared by rounding The Manacles east cardinal buoy. Like Portland Bill, overfalls extend 2½NM south of Lizard Point and we set a waypoint 3NM south to give them a reasonable margin. From here we set a virtually due-west course for St Mary's, passing about 2NM south of the Wolf Rock light house at 1500 where we met another yacht. The wind then dropped to 8 knots, so we motor-sailed from 1100. The low-lying island of St Mary's came into view at 1700 and we arrived at our waypoint, the Spanish Ledge east cardinal buoy

Peninnis Head lighthouse

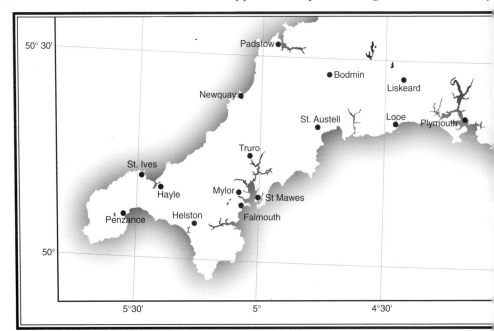

at 1815, crossing St Mary's Sound to round the western extremity of St Mary's, Garrison Hill, and enter St Mary's Pool on a leading line defined by two white beacons on Mount Flagon. We then moored to a vacant visitor's mooring. The Pool has five trots of moorings on smart colour-coded buoys, yellow for visitors.

ST MARY'S

St Mary's is the private harbour of the Duchy of Cornwall. We hope this brief Skippers' information will be useful for exploring one of the worlds most beautiful archipelagos anchored in blue Atlantic water.

Please note that St Mary's Harbour is particularly vulnerable to gales from the North West. Weather conditions can also change and deteriorate very rapidly. All yacht skippers are responsible for their vessels. If the weather deteriorates when you are in the harbour, think of seeking alternative shelter early. Only a few quayside berths will be made available owing to the daily arrival of the ferry and cargo vessels.

The harbour office is situated on the quay. The Harbour Master can be contacted out of working hours (emergency only please) Telephone: 423343.

Moorings

There are 38 new deep water yacht moorings - 'YELLOW' buoys. Please contact the Harbour Master for advice. Visitors are NOT to take up local residents moorings.

Anchorage

All other craft are NOT to anchor seaward of the Lifeboat and HM Customs Buoys. This is the turning area for the ferry and cargo vessels on a daily basis. Also KEEP CLEAR of RNLI slipway.

Water Taxi

CH16 (working channel 11) call sign "APOLLO".

Tidal Information

Chart datum is LAT which is 2.91 metres below ordnance datum. This is considerably affected by wind conditions and barometric pressure.

Leisure Activities

Gig Racing: Takes place on Wednesday and Friday evenings and normally terminates at St Mary's Quay. Spectators and craft are advised to keep clear of the race area. World Championship is on May Day (UK) Bank Holiday.

St Mary's moorings

Falmouth

Isles of Scilly

Tuesday 2 June

Beautiful morning with occasional shower. Good shower facilities(£1 for 8 minutes) on the quay. Mike took the 1130 flight for Penzance and would be back in Ipswich at 1930! We brought BABAJI alongside the harbour wall after fuelling at 30p/litre and taking on water at 50p a fill. I updated the CA website from harbourmaster's office. We shopped for provisions in the supermarket in Hugh Town. Hugh Town is well served with shops, mostly geared to the needs of tourists.

St Mary's Porth Hellick Bay

St Mary's Porth Hellick Bay

Robin Mawer, the CA's HLR at St Mary's, who had arranged for me to use the harbourmaster's telephone socket, came on board for a drink. They are still talking about the MV Cito that ran onto St Mary's in March 1997 (on autopilot with the watchkeeper asleep!) bringing dozens of containers of tyres (all the island's cars have new tyres), sports clothes, computer parts (thousands of mice!) etc and have recently had approval that they can keep their spoil!

St Mary's Porth Hellick Bay

ST MARY'S (ISLES OF SCILLY)

The 38 'new' yellow visitors' buoys and many new green locals' buoys make anchoring in any real shelter impossible, while most of the yellow buoys are highly exposed to the Atlantic swell. Distance between buoys is 15m and allows unoccupied down-wind buoys to bump against yachts of 10m length at LW. But harbour is very popular, especially with the French.

Falmouth

Isles of Scilly

ST MARY'S TO CROSSHAVEN (CORK)

Wednesday/Thursday 3/4 June

(Charts 1123, 2049,1765, 1777). 139 NM, 27 hours 45 minutes

Crosshaven

Very uncomfortable night with the NNE wind holding us abeam to Atlantic swell entering the harbour. We noticed that unused moorings were bumping yachts on upwind moorings at LW, a point to note when selecting one of the 38 visitors' buoys. The roll gradually builds up until you almost fall off the bunk, then dies away before repeating the cycle. Dick Blamey has been diving in each morning, so Margo and I tried in the shallow Porth Hellick bay and found this not too bad. We came alongside the wall again, when the 0535 forecast gave no indication of an early change from the NNE headwind we would encounter, and had a lovely walk past the Peninnis Head lighthouse and airstrip to Porth Hellick. The footpath crosses the end of the runway which ends abruptly over a small cliff, and has traffic lights to warn walkers of the approach of an aircraft.

The north wind was much lighter by the 1755 shipping forecast which at last gave a wind becoming SE, so we got away at 1815. Excellent visibility showed Scillies at their best as we finally cleared the last hazard, the little island Mincarla. It became calm around sunset at 2130 with an uncomfortable residual swell, but the SE wind began before a spectacular

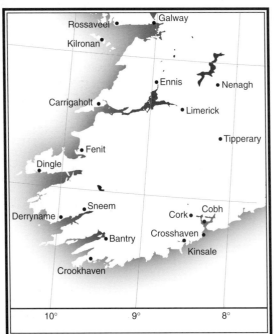

28

sunrise with many brilliantly lit trails across the sky. I cut the engine at 0930, and got Concorde's sonic double boom to full effect while fitting the jib pole to hold out the genoa! Although I have heard this boom many times it never fails to shock!

I called two ships approaching from our port beam on a steady bearing to ensure they were aware of our presence. The crew were most impressed! We cleared the Kinsale Head gas rigs at 1440 and sighted land at 1615. With the wind dropping, we motored into Cork harbour, berthing on a Royal Cork Yacht Club pontoon at 2200, with time to do the Murphy/Beamish comparison at the friendly YC bar. This is the world's oldest yacht club, although it moved from its elegant building in Cork to this more convenient site with modern facilities, spacious bars, and with its own pontoons at Crosshaven in the Owenboy River. The club was in feverish activity in preparation for Cork Week, for which 650 yachts and racing dinghies were expected. Rock infill was being used to increase the foreshore area in front of the club, a canvas village was being set up, and new pontoons were being installed. Our crew left us here; from now on we were a husband and wife crew

CROSSHAVEN

Crosshaven (Cork harbour) the world's first YC, the Royal Cork, was as friendly as ever. Rock infill has been used to increase foreshore area in front of the Club, and pontoons were being extended to nearly double the marina capacity, in readiness for Cork Week, otherwise little had changed since 1981. RCYC started the 1720 Class (1720 is year of their foundation) rather like the Melge). Expensive (£16/day for 31 to 35ft) but includes showers and electricity. Small shops but no bank in Crosshaven. This is the best entry port from SW England or Scillies with safe deep water and good shelter. Banks, cash dispenser and supermarket at Carrigaline 5M along Owenboy River (past Drake's Pool where Drake hid his squadron when out-numbered by the Spanish enemy in 1580). Diesel at Crosshaven Boat Yard Marina 30p/litre.

Crosshaven Marina

A comprehensive range of facilities for yachts up to 140' X 14' draught includes swinging moorings, fuel and water supplies, full service facilities and mains electricity. On-site boatyard engineering facilities and expertise include welding and machinery in stainless steel, aluminium and bronze, repairs and maintenance to hulls/rigging, routine and detailed engine maintenance. Bareboat and skippered yacht charters are also organised. Salve Marine provides a personal and helpful service at a competitive price. Contact: Tel: 021-831145 Fax: 021-831747.

ROYAL CORK YACHT CLUB

Founded in 1720, this is the oldest yacht club in the world,and also the largest club on the South Coast of Ireland - known worldwide as host to the biennial Ford Cork Week Regatta, proof of its vitality and expertise. The RCYC runs a very full programme of events right throughout the year. In 1998 the highlight was Ford Cork Week. Quoting Yachting World: 'It's the best run, organised, social friendly event - you name it - you can't say enough good things about it'. On alternate years the club organises Heineken Dinghy Week, in 1997 incorporating the Laser 11 World Championship as well as many National Championships. Crosshaven village is well served with Bed and Breakfasts and a variety of restaurants all within walking distance. Tel: 021-831023 Fax:021-831586.

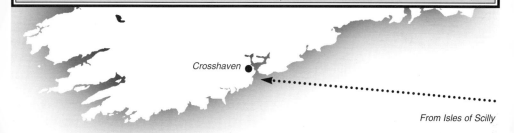

Crosshaven

From Isles of Scilly

CROSSHAVEN TO KINSALE

Friday 5 June - Free day in Crosshaven

Crosshaven has a few small shops but no bank. We therefore cycled five miles along a path beside the Owenboy River and Drake's Pool where Drake successfully hid his fleet from the much larger marauding Spanish fleet in 1580, to Carrigoline, an attractive market town with excellent supermarkets and banks with cash dispensers.

Kinsale up river and marina

Saturday 6 June, Crosshaven to Kinsale

(Charts 1777, 1765). 17NM, 6 hours

Kinsale stands on the north bank of the River Bandon estuary, but is hidden - and well sheltered - by a U-turn in the river. Before approaching from the west the Bulman south cardinal is rounded, giving clearance from the submerged Bulman Rock. The magnificent and vast star shaped Charles Fort, standing on rock headland with walls down to the sea, then comes into view on the west side.

Kinsale down the Bandon river

Once past Monet Point on the eastern side the smaller James Fort appears. These two forts must have provided terrific protection from any insurgents. Two port hand buoys, Spur and Spit, take us close below Charles Fort and clear of the Blockhouse Point before we see the welcoming marina, although unlike many English estuaries there is still plenty of room to anchor.

When we arrived the harbourmaster greeted us with a long-term forecast of force 8 on Monday, 9 (strong gale) on Tuesday,

8 on Wednesday, and advised against going into one of the anchorages on Sunday as these are exposed. We should really have left on that Sunday window, but after all people do come to Kinsale on holiday, so we decided to enjoy a rest. We used the Met Office service and spoke to a forecaster (£17) who confirmed the dismal three-day forecast, although not with force 8/9! Nevertheless we had to wait here for four days. However nearly all the other yachts there were waiting too and there were few arrivals - mostly charter boats with deadlines to return.

We swam briefly in Sandy Cove (2 miles away), but at low water it was very shallow. We got wet again cycling back in heavy rain. We had seen it the previous night at high water while Margo was painting in Kinsale. Two teenagers were diving in off the sea wall.

KINSALE HARBOUR

Kinsale Marina: £14 (first two nights, then £11) for 9m including electricity; showers £1. Very friendly YC with good food modestly priced. Attractive town with supermarket, banks, bookshop, etc. This is a natural harbour formed by the estuary of the Bandon River. The LUSITANIA was torpedoed off the Old Head of Kinsale on 7th May 1915, with the loss of 1,198 lives. It was a determining factor in the USA joining forces with the Allies against Germany. In 1601 some of the Spanish Armada landed at Kinsale. The Spanish fleet consisted of 3,000 men; reduced by adversity from a force of 6,000, they were far too weak to withstand the subsequent blockade of the harbour by the Anglo-Irish Privy Council. Irish chieftains O'Neill and O'Donnell decided to lend what strength they could to the Spanish. The ensuing battles led to many Irish being killed. The town of Kinsale is now known for its hospitality and international cuisine.

Kinsale is 18 miles from Cork city and 13 miles from Cork Airport. A bus service departs for the city centre terminus and collects at the airport en route. Castlepark from the town centre is 1.5 miles by road or five minutes by ferry which operates from the Trident Hotel to Castlepark Marina during the high season.

Our three clear days gave plenty of time for exploration by bicycle. We visited Charles Fort which is undergoing excellent restorative work to its former glory, and where Margo found time for some painting. Built in 1677 it continued to be garrisoned until 1922. On another day we visited the more ruinous James Fort commanding an excellent view from one side across the river to Charles Fort and on the other side across the river to Kinsale. We went by the long road bridge and returned by ferry. We also visited St Multose Church, built in 1190 and one of Ireland's oldest churches. It was here that Charles II was proclaimed King by Prince Rupert. Kinsale also has many small and attractively painted shops along its narrow streets.

Kinsale is renowned for its culinary expertise, with many internationally-known restaurants, and hosts an annual gourmet festival. Our meals were confined to humbler but excellent sea food with good company in the restaurant upstairs in the Yacht Club.

Crosshaven

Kinsale

KINSALE TO CROOKHAVEN

Thursday 11 June,

(Charts 1795, 2681, 2092). 60 NM, 11 hours 45m.

The 0525 forecast gave NE 6-7 decreasing 4-5, mainly fair, visibility mainly good, so we left at 0715 which gave the beginning of the ebb at Old Head of Kinsale. Giving the overfalls south of the Old Head a half-mile margin we set a direct course for Toe Head; this took us close to Seven Heads and Galley Head with its off-lying Doolic Rock, and well off the coast, crossing Clonakilty and Glandore Bays.

Old head of Kinsale lighthouse

We rounded Toe Head through Stag Sound and north of The Stags, a group of pretty fearsome looking precipitous rocks. We sailed for a while with a double reefed main and five rolls in the genoa but soon motor-sailed to make the most of this offshore wind. We rounded Clear Island, as the tide would have turned against us in Gascanane Sound. It then became rough as the fetch for the North wind increased to about 10 miles and combined with the Atlantic swell which we'd had all day. Fastnet Rock appeared looking like an approaching frigate from the east until becoming unmistakably Fastnet. Two yachts that had passed us earlier had rounded Fastnet and were on their way home. Fortunately we had rounded the Fastnet in 1991 so didn' feel the urge to do this again.

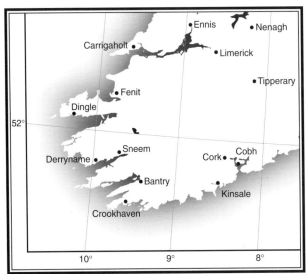

The sea gradually subsided a we approached Crookhaven and Margo emerged to han sails in the entrance. There ar now many visitors' buoys o the village and we decided t take one. Unfortunately the strops dangle from the buoys and are almost impossible to pick up with a boathook from the height of our foredeck; a neighbouring yachtsman saw our plight and valiantly rowed over (in a 20 plus knot wind) to attach a rope to the strop which he handed to us. With the spring tide HW and strong wind it took both of us to get the strop attached.

We were amazed to see GRUMPY SKIPPER, whose mooring we had used in Bosham, and joined them for a drink in the local overlooking the harbour! There is a convenient mini-harbour here with a beach at LW and steps where a dinghy may be left safely.

The evening shipping forecast gave the wind going round to the SE, just right to round Mizen Head tomorrow and make some progress northwards on the morrow.

CROOKHAVEN

Excellent shelter. Moorings £5/night but difficult to pick up as bridles are not buoyed, and hang below buoys. Friendly pub will sell items from the adjacent shop out of shop hours. A fine harbour which can be entered at all states of the tide. It has good shelter from all but E to SE winds.

Approach

From the Fastnet Rock steer North to fetch the entrance. Give Alderman Rocks and Black Horse Rocks a good berth. You can anchor in the North East corner or off the quays. Several visitors' moorings are available at approximately £5. per night. Water is available from both piers. Beware of kelp and in parts holding is only moderate.

Kinsale

Crookhaven

▲ Fastnet Rock

Friday 12 June

(Charts 2129, 2184, 2552, 1840). 23 NM, 5 hours 25 minutes

The forecasts for sea areas Fastnet and for the Shannon differed but both soon became west 5 to 7. We made passage plans for the Sneem (Kenmare River) and Lawrence Cove on Bere Island in Bantry Bay, planning to get a feel for conditions as we rounded Mizen Head. However I felt quite tired after 12 hours of sailing yesterday, and the weather was a bit too miserable for an anchorage, so knowing Lawrence Cove had diesel, we opted for the latter.

Lawrence Cove Marina

We rounded Mizen Head on the last of the flood so the sea was not too bad. We passed Three Castles Head with its white Ardnakinna Lighthouse at the we entrance to Berehaven and it was clear at 9 NM but the visibility closed in and aft

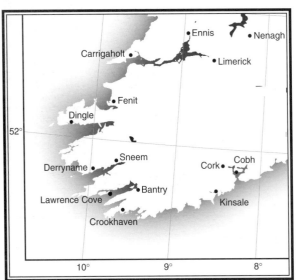

mooring the north bank Berehaven was obscured, I alone the mountains. GRUM SKIPPER and SUKANUK had al left for Lawrence Cove a t before us at 0815, but we g there first and helped them mo

The very friendly marina h opened in June 1997 and be considerably extended duri the winter. For our 9.5 me length it was £10/night pl showers (new, very clean), £1 diesel 30p/litre, electricity a water on pontoons. It provic excellent shelter from all wi directions. Other facilities included telephone and village store and a post office in Rennin village, a ten minute walk away. The marina should be called surprise or secret marina as it is, the extreme SW corner of the cove, doesn't appear until the last minute, and if you didn't know it was there you would have turned back as the depth fell! About 20 yachts were here. Lawrence Cove Marina qualifies for four stars. It is privately owned by a couple that are really putting themselves into it.

We walked into the village in the rain. This was to be our first day without any sunshine, and only 14°C at midday. June?

The shop in the village takes you back 50 years, with its mahogany counter and the assistants and all the stock on shelves behind! The newspapers come in at 11am and can be reserved. There was no GSM signal in the marina so I had to walk about half a mile up a hill (when the rain had stopped) to find some shade to see the laptop screen. I felt like an enemy agent crouching behind a wall! Saturday was pretty wild but we had an excellent and mountainous cycle ride across Bere Island (which remained a British base until 1938 and still has camp buildings in excellent order - there are clearly no vandals here). We should be spelling it "bere" and not "bear" as in British publications; it has no connection with bears! It was called Beerehaven in a map of 1599.

Saturday 13 June Rest day on Bere Island

Actually it wasn't much of a rest as we determined to explore the island on our bicycles. We had a little map that showed what looked like a good path up the spine of the island, but found it hard going carrying the bikes at times. We were rewarded with splendid views from the hill tops and descended to pick up the coast road on its north side to return. Watched the ferry from the mainland arrive and depart with holiday makers on foot or with bikes.

LAWRENCE COVE

Lawrence Cove Marina is tucked in the extreme SE corner of Lawrence Cove, Bere Island in Bantry Bay. It appears at the last moment but therefore provides excellent shelter. Electricity, water and diesel on pontoons. Very friendly owners. £10/night for 9.5m. Showers £1. Card phone. Diesel 30p/litre. Position on pontoon: Lat: 51° 38'.0N Long: 9° 49'. 9.W. Shop/PO 10 minutes. Lawrence Cove on Bere Island is a wonderful place. There is good anchorage and a good local pub at Rerrin to eat and drink. Make sure you ask the local fishermen to sell you some shellfish. An alternative destination from Lawrence Cove could be to Portmagee, 38nm. The journey is a full day's trip out around Dursey Head, past The Bull, past Scarrif Island, Puffin Island and into Portmagee. Portmagee has a safe anchorage and is a lovely town. Valentia Island and its wonderful gardens are worth a visit. If you want to visit the Great Skellig it is best to take a ferry out from Portmagee. The Fisherman's Bar serves good good and drink and there is also a small supermarket for some provisions.

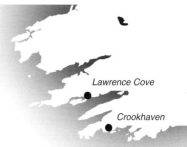

Lawrence Cove

Crookhaven

LAWRENCE COVE TO SNEEM AND DERRYNANE

Sunday 14th June

(Charts 1840, 2495).
45 NM, 9 hrs 20 mins total

Left our comfortable cove at 0945 and again passed the wreck of the Klondyker BARDINE REEFER. Apparently this was impounded after the Russian owners failed to pay debts, the crew remaining unpaid and near starvation. It was then sold to a new owner who didn't want the crew, and it was set on fire in mysterious circumstances. It is an eyesore near the middle of the main channel. Passed through the narrow (1^1/$_2$ cable) west entrance back into Bantry Bay, rounding the Black Ball and White Ball (why so called?) Heads, then round Cro Island before turning North into Dursey Sound. This is remarkable as the northe

Derrynane landing

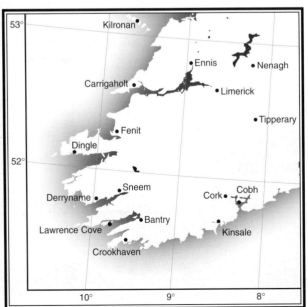

exit, under a cable car, is n seen until one is practically the north shore. Since we we only just off Springs (whi give a 4 knot stream) we h checked carefully the start the west-going stream (1h 35 after HW Cobh) in the Iri Coast Pilot (NP40) and pass through 3 hours later, touchi 10 knots at the narrowest po under the cable car. Then round Cod's Head into t Kenmare estuary.

Because a northerly wind w forecast we went first nor east to Sneem harbour (whi was really lovely and whe ve anchored for a while - we wish we'd stayed but local knowledge is required to nchor within rowing distance of the hotel) then west to Derrynane. Here we nchored in a tiny harbour after a terrifying entrance between rocks using a leading ine with plain concrete beacons that could almost be buildings. Some red and white aint would do wonders for the confidence of first-time visitors!

Ve had had the best forecast from the Wet Office (as the Irish call it) for some days, ut it blew up as we entered the harbour and was still 20 knots gusting over 25 knots s we anchored. We hoped it would quieten before we turned in, but at least the nchor had bit very reassuringly.

DERRYNANE TO SNEEM

Derrynane has a narrow entrance between rocks. Leading marks are two whitish brick structures with pointed tops. Good holding in sand near "cliff" but check depth. Saw a yacht fouling an old anchor at S side. Many moorings at E side.

Sneem is idyllic (when fine!), and has good shelter and holding off beach at W end. The Kenmare River is a large beautiful inlet which extends about 28 miles ENE and is 7.5 miles wide.The land on either side is mountainous and the scenery is magnificent and a contrast to the previous two days. There are numerous harbours and anchorages and Sneem is 16 miles up this river. Ballycrovane harbour, Ardgroom harbour, Collorus harbour and West cove are all nice places to visit in addition or as an alternative to Sneem. Parkinsilla Hotel overlooks the anchorage and is a good place to have a lovely meal. There are a couple of good friendly pubs with live sessions and plenty of Guinness.

SNEEM TO CASTLETOWN BEREHAVEN

Sneem to Castletown Berehaven is a lovely sail passing out of the Kenmare river around Dursey Head and into Bantry Bay. It is tempting to motor through Dursey Sound, a narrow passage between Dursey Island and mainland but this should only be done in calm weather sticking strictly to the directions in the cruising guide. Castletown is one of the major fishing ports on the west coast and is a lively town well worth a visit. There are plenty of pubs and restaurants to choose from and lots of wonderful walking along the coast and up in the mountains. Diesel, water and gas can be bought here, along with all the provisions you should need.There is sheltered anchorage in the harbour, a couple of visitors' moorings and a place on the west quay for yachts to go alongside. MacCarthy's bar is good for a hot meal and excellent traditional music.

Derrynane landing leading mark

Derrynane   Sneem

Lawrence Cove

DERRYNANE TO DINGLE

Monday 15 June

(Charts 2495, 2789, CA Hbk). 35 NM, 8 hours 15 minutes

Glorious morning. We rowed over to the little pier below the leading mark, and walked up a steep zigzag road giving magnificent views over the harbour and outlying islands with Dursey Island in the distance. No wonder holiday homes are popular here with their huge picture windows. We saw two further planning permission forms posted

Entering Dingle

in lovely unspoilt spots and hope this isn't going to become a continuous village. We returned to find GRUMF SKIPPER getting ready to depart, but as they had fouled their anchor they were not much ahead when we left at 1100.

Three headlands were rounded: Bolus, Canduff and Bray with fine mountains inland. Dingle marina is in a well-sheltered but shallow natural harbour. A dredged channel has an almost 90° bend around a covered sand bank so it is important to identify and follow the buoys. An amenities block was scheduled for opening in July. This delightful town even boasts a cybercafe, which was fully utilized when we visited, while Walkers Pub or "The Hole in the Wall" claims to be Ireland's first Internet Pub. But Walkers is kept the old way, no fancy decorations or furniture. Just a typical Irish pub with plenty of taps for Guinness!

Bray Head

Dingle Marina

DINGLE

Dingle Marina has a new facilities block due for opening mid-July. 9.5m cost £10/night. Diesel 30p/l. Slip for drying out. Dingleweb cafe £5/hour or £1.50/15 min.

Approach:

The entrance is straightforward but narrow. The channel is dredged and buoyed and you may be met by the friendly local dolphin. There are many opportunities for cultural activities plus a beautiful landscape. You can visit Blasket Island while in Dingle. There is an anchorage off the Great Blasket but it should only be used in light winds and especially not in northerly winds. It is an amazing island and if at all possible it should not be missed. Ventry Bay is also a good place to anchor for lunch. It is only an hour sail from Dingle and has a shop, pub and restaurant. Ventry beach is ideal for walking or swimming. There are loads of places to go on the final night in Dingle. Greany's restaurant, John Doyles or Beginish are excellent places to eat, followed by Dick Mac's, An Droicead Bead or Maire de Barra for a pint or two. Portmagee is also a short sail away from Dingle - 7nm.

Dingle

Derrynane

DINGLE TO FENIT

Wednesday 17 June

(Charts 2789, 2254). 41 NM, 9 hours

Left at 0600 after a just tolerable wind forecast; if we'd been put off by every forecast of winds of 5 to 7 we'd have made little progress this year! Having missed seeing the dolphin Funghe, Dingle's special tourist attraction, on the way in, we were rewarded by

Fenit marina and bridge

not one, but four dolphins gambolling around us as we left, a grand send-off. Later one kept close company while the others cavorted across the bay and we assumed this was Funghe. We also saw several puffins. Our departure was timed to pass north through the Blasket Sound on the last of the north-going stream and gave a SMG of 7kts. Once round Sybil Pt, our most westerly point in Ireland (10°30'W) the wind increased to its forecast range of force 5 to 7 SE, and despite the lee shore became uncomfortable. Our attempts to close with the cliffs were thwarted by salmon nets and I just stopped in time to avoid over-running one, the owners in the fishing boat either oblivious of us or unconcerned - normally they wave vigorously as the next one did. Their seaward ends were at least 2.5NM offshore.

The sea died as we rounded Brandon Point and passed through Magharee Sound with the Seven Hogs Islands to port. Entered the new Fenit Harbour marina. This is connected to Fenit village by a viaduct 6 cables long, with a small shop at its foot and excellent store a little further on the right. It has 110 berths including 40 for visitors, and plenty of room. Charge £1/metre/night min £10 including excellent showers but electricity requires a prepaid £1 card. Got soaked cycling into the village and Margo fell off her bike after getting stuck in an old rail track along the viaduct, so altogether it was not a very happy venture! Filled up with diesel at only 22p/litre on the quay within the marina.

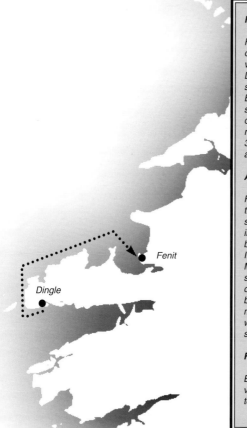

FENIT HARBOUR MARINA

Fenit (Tralee Bay) has a new enclosed marina built on to the old pierhead one mile out to sea on a viaduct. Metered electricity and water on pontoons. Diesel alongside inner wall (22p/l) Card-operated security gate. Free showers. Harbour Master: David Buttimer. Small shop at foot of pier and comprehensive shop a little further on on the right that will deliver to boat (Tel: 066 36151). Several good restaurants including West End Bar (Tel: 066 36246). OK to leave boat here. A well sheltered anchorage in all winds except south east.

Approach:

Fenit lies on the E side of Tralee Bay, but be aware that entering the bay is not straightforward. Make sure you consult your chart carefully before entering. The SW coast of Ireland offers some of the best sailing and the best selection of marinas in Irish waters. The best of these is Fenit Harbour Marina. The 110-berth marina has berths for all sizes of boats from 6m to 15m, in minimum water depth of 3m CD, with one berth capable of taking boats up to 30m. There is access in all tides, with minimum depth of 5m CD in the approaches. As well as all the usual facilities, the marina has video surveillance and a smart card access gate.

Facilities:

Electricity, water, fuel, crane, security gate and video surveillance, showers, toilets, laundry, telephone, facilities for disabled.

FENIT TO CARRIGAHOLT

Thursday 18 June

(Charts 2254,1819). 25 NM, 5 hours 30 minutes

Wind forecast today SSW5/6 increasing S/SSE 6/7. Set off in 20knots but this fell to 5 so we had to motor. At least 12 dolphins saw us off from Fenit, but wisely remained in the sheltered water. Sketched the panama hat shaped Mucklaghmore rock, 30 metres high, as we passed it in the middle of the exit from Tralee Bay. Rounded the

Carrigaholt pier from our anchorage

smooth grassy-topped Kerry Head into the broad Shannon Estuary with Loop Head clearly visible 7 NM to the north.

It is difficult to count the dolphins for they spend most of the time submerged and can then emerge all around you, but we estimated we had

20 to welcome us into the Shannon. They drove the echosounder mad (was it perhaps attracting them?) so I turned it off. The other excitement was a helicopter flying very low over us and practically giving me a heart attack - I thought at first a power boat must be about to collide with us.

The Shannon got very rough with the wind against tide as it narrowed at Kilcredaun Heads, so instead of proceeding to Kilrush we anchored in 3 metres round the corner off Carrigaholt Pier, well out of the tide. Stopping here saved us a further 7NM to Kilrush (and back the next day) with its lock and an expensive marina. We had good holding out of the stream and a quiet night. Margo painted the castle from the boat so we didn't need to go ashore, although Tom Pilkington commented in an email that the mussels on the pier are excellent! The sun was actually shining (2045hrs) at last.

CARRIGAHOLT

'Excellent anchorage in shelter of pier in mouth of Shannon, saves going on to expensive Kilrush marina with inconvenience of lock. Pick your own mussels from pier.' **Tom Pilkington,** email.

Carrigaholt is in a wide bay about 1½m north of Kilcredaun Point at the entrance to the River Shannon. It is well sheltered from the S through W to N. If you plan to go far into the bay to anchor off the Old Quay beware the soundings which date from 1842.

Approach: The mouth of the Shannon is approximately 11m wide. It is well lit and all dangers are marked. In strong NW through W to S winds there is a bad race during the ebb. Give both heads a good berth.

There are good facilities, about ten minutes walk from the New Quay in the village of Carrigaholt. There is a fine new marina at Kilrush Creek. And if you wish to go further the wet docks at Limerick can be entered.

Carrigaholt

Fenit

CARRIGAHOLT TO KILRONAN
(Inishmore, Aran Islands)

Friday 19 June

(Charts 2254, (3338). 3339) 50NM, 9 hrs 45 mins

Forecast of 4/5 occasionally 6, so we set off with one reef in the main and mizzen. We again saw dolphins, but these showed no interest. (What do they do at night? Do they sleep?) Rounded Loop Head, a lovely grassy headland over cliffs. The cliff has strata folding down to the sea giving a polished appearance. Loop Head is the intended site for a vital aerial for the new Loran-C navigation chain, but difficulty with planning permission has delayed this for years. Having rounded Loop Head we turned NE and had a splendid run with 6 knots SMG for some hours. The wind peaked at 21 knots by which time we had 8 rolls in the genoa to keep things manageable in the Atlantic swell. We heard a Mayday from a fishing boat with an anchor not holding but the Galway lifeboat was with them in 2 minutes to tow them off!

Inishmore - a rocky island

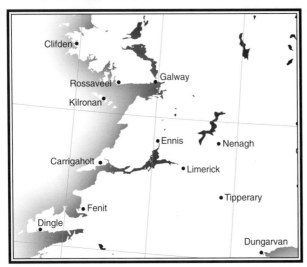

The sea became very rough as we approached the Aran Islands, but the 1NM wide Gregory Sound was fortunately clearly visible, as it looks very narrow from a distance. Waves breaking against the cliffs were sending spray up about 30 metres. Luckily it got quieter in Gregory Sound before becoming really tranquil in Killeany Bay. We anchored in 3 metres south of Kilronan slip, took our bicycles ashore in the dinghy, and cycled to the Iron Age Dun Aengus fort (thought to be around 1st century and one of finest of its type in Europe), 3 miles away plus a 20 minute uphill walk. The outer fortified area is of 14 acres. The central area is surrounded by three massive walls and an unusual chevaux de frise of sharply pointed stones facing upwards around it, which must have been a formidable obstacle for potential attackers. The south side is 'bounded' by a precipitous 300 foot drop to the foaming sea below. An eccentric young man was leaning into the wind standing on a rock outcrop overlooking the sea! We returned to a super sea food chowder at the Dun Aenghasa restaurant overlooking the bay. Highly recommended.

We returned to find the dinghy missing and experienced a moment of panic but some teenagers had just taken it to the other side of the pier, bless them.

KILRONAN

Approach: *Pass through North Sound between Goruma Island and Inishmore. Temple Benan ruin in the SSW corner of bay in line with the sand patch 226° leads into the bay in confidence leaving the con buoy to starboard. Steer over to starboard towards the pier. There are good facilities including diesel, water, groceries, pub, ferry and air services to Galway. Don't miss the 1st century fort at Dunaengus.*

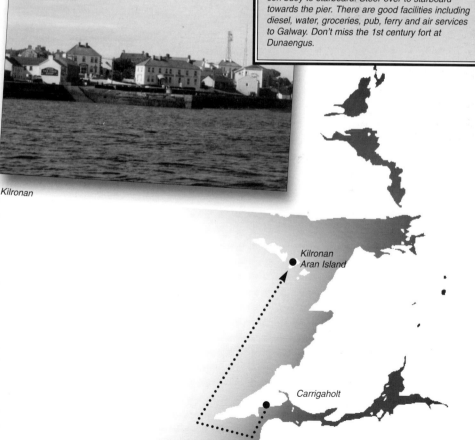

Kilronan

Kilronan
Aran Island

Carrigaholt

KILRONAN TO GALWAY DOCK

Saturday 20 June

(Charts 3339, 1984). 25 NM, 5 hours

A perfect morning, but no wind. We had an extremely smooth passage east to Galway Dock arriving shortly after the gates had opened (HW-2). We had to wait while a large trawler came out very slowly, and were called on VHF by Frank Sheridan, our HLR, who was on board! He had left our mail in the gate machinery room. I was pleased to see that a Lister engine, almost identical to our boat engine, was used to provide emergency power for operating the gates. The need to leave before HW+2 when the gates would close again gave us little time other than for shopping. We found a splendid shopping mall with good shops. We were not to know that further bad weather was going to keep us gale-bound at our next point and give the opportunity to return by bus.

Galway Dock, BABAJI moored by machinery room

GALWAY DOCK TO CASHLA BAY

Saturday 20 June

(Charts 3339). 23 NM, 4 hours 40 minutes

Leaving Galway just before gates closed at HW, we had an easy run against a light headwind allowing me to type an email under way (for first time). We moored alongside ARAN FLYER overnight, having been told (wrongly) that the fishing harbour was out-of-bounds for yachts.

Galway

Third largest city in the Republic of Ireland with good connections to Dublin and other parts of the country.Galway Dock - Harbour Master is Frank Sheridan, CA HLR. Near excellent shops surrounded by luxury flats like Limehouse. The harbour is very much commercial with coasters calling frequently and a ferry to the Aran Islands. The dock lock gates open at HW - 2h to HW. There is a dedicated area for small craft in the S W part of the basin. The HM is very helpful and can be contacted on Tel: (091) 62329. West Galway Bay Sailing Club is usually open at weekends. (091) 84527. There is water on the quay and plenty of supplies in town. Facilities are available including repairs to engines, hull and electronics.

Approach:

The Aran Islands break the Westerly swell but due to its size the bay is fairly exposed. If making for the dock you will find it well lit and buoyed to show dredged channels.

Galway

Kilronan
Aran Island

GALWAY DOCK TO ROSSAVEEL (Cashla Bay)

Sunday 21 June

We set off at 0800 but found the bay rough and met a French yacht entering. They called out that it was gusting 35 knots and they had split their mainsail en route from Galway. We thus decided to turn back and read while anchored, with the mizzen reducing roll. The French yacht later entered the fishing harbour so we lay alongside it, rafted against an interesting engineless sailing vessel with an open hold and rock ballast, and five fishing vessels, 11 to walk across in total. Visited a ghastly local pub modelled on an American road house.

Alongside ARAN FLYER in Cashla Bay

Monday 22 June

We were delayed by fuelling and le at 1115. After battling for two hour into a 25 knot headwind and roug sea (and still in lee of the Ara Islands to the south) I asked mysel why do we cruise? To enjoy eve changing scenery? (Fog!) Sailing (Making 3 knots motor-sailing into rough sea!) Outdoor living? (Heav rain!) We U-turned and sailed back at 7 knots feeling somewhat sheepish as our French neighbours took our warps again. We had an excellent hot shower while a fish auction was in progress. Met the manager and founder of the fisherman's cooperative, who was born in Hitchin! The fish used to go to Dublin for auction and then be sent back to Galway; he started selling locally, making more money by staying ashore, then started an auction in Galway before getting £15m investment here to reclaim land and build a new quay with 4m at LW, an ice plant and auction hall. Gale warning for tomorrow, so BABAJI is stuck again.

CASHLA BAY

Rossaveel Harbour in Cashla Bay is an excellent all-weather harbour. Lie alongside disused trawlers or anchor in the bay. No charge. Water hoses. Diesel 23.2p/l at old pier end, or phone garage for delivery Tel: 572169. Shower. £15m invested in harbour and facilities in recent years; home to 23 trawlers. Harbour Master Capt. John Connolley, very helpful. One of the most sheltered anchorages on this part of the coast. It is lit with two fixed lights and several lit and unlit buoys.

Approach: Entry is possible in practically all weather conditions. Take care not to enter Greatman's Bay by mistake (see your chart). There is a small shop and a pub at Rossaveel with diesel and water available. At Struthan on the other side you will find shops, a hotel, telephone and a bus to Galway. Fuel and water on quay.

ROSSAVEEL TO CLIFDEN

Wednesday 24 June

(Charts 3339, 1820). 45NM, 10 hours

The forecast was for SW-W 4/5 becoming 5/6, so we set off at 10, leaving our French neighbours waiting for a north wind. Third time lucky, at last we were out o Rossaveel, not one of Ireland's more attractive or interesting ports. We were relieved to pass Slyne Head, thus accomplishing another major headland hurdle. We kept : NM off and it wasn't too bad, with long Atlantic rollers of about 3m and not too rough

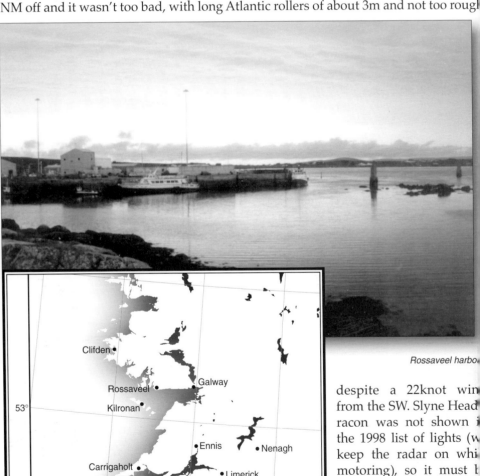

Rossaveel harbo

despite a 22knot win from the SW. Slyne Head racon was not shown i the 1998 list of lights (w keep the radar on whi motoring), so it must b new. We anchored in 8m i Clifden, a pretty natur harbour, near the sailing club building and RNLI slip but didn't go ashore. After a rough passage followed by a quiet anchorage it is often more relaxing to stay on board. The rough seas here make it impracticable to tow a tender, so going ashore involves inflating it, heaving it overboard, sponging it dry, fitting the bracket for the outboard, and lowering the heavy outboard from the pushpit, then reversing all this on return. When anchored close to the shore the outboard is not needed, but even so launching and recovery is tiring after a long day.

Rossaveel harbour at low water

Clifden

Rossaveel

CLIFDEN

It is not worth the hassle of crossing the bar and wending up to the village unless holed-up. Good overnight anchorage off sailing club and RNLI slip. The bay is a sheltered natural harbour. Beware of the numerous fish farms.

Approach: *Use caution and your echo sounder as the bar may be silting up. There is a second bar at the entrance to Ardbear Bay. The head of the bay has good shelter if you give the shore a fair berth.*

CLIFDEN TO INISHBOFIN

Thursday 25 June

(Chart 1820). 17NM, 3 hours 36 minutes

We chickened out of the High Island Sound inshore passage but the sea off High Island was horrendous and we'd have done better inside. The Atlantic rollers meet the seabed rising from 75 metres depth to vertical cliffs in only 3 cables, and doubtless

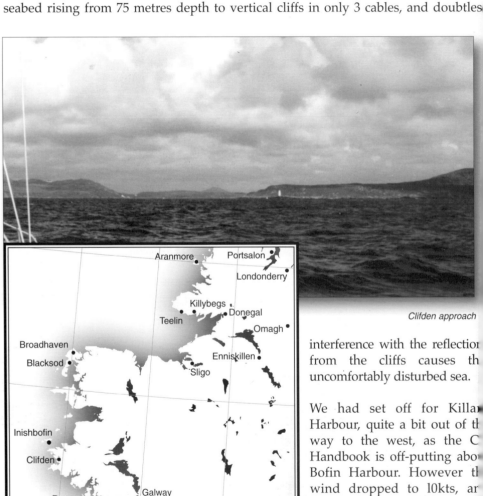

Clifden approach

interference with the reflection from the cliffs causes the uncomfortably disturbed sea.

We had set off for Killary Harbour, quite a bit out of the way to the west, as the C Handbook is off-putting abou Bofin Harbour. However th wind dropped to 10kts, and once clear of the breakers of Cuddoo Rock it looked place to the North so we made fo

Inishbofin and had a smooth entry and quick anchoring near the Royal Cruising Club yacht ALBUERA before lunch.

Ashore at the pier we walked to a beach of lovely white sand and shells in sheltered Rusheen Bay with an azure sea but the temperature wasn't living up to its appearance. We had a quick refreshing bathe and then back to the little shop beside Day's bar for provisions, its limited stock all on shelves behind a heavy wooden counter. Then had a good fish and chips meal in Day's Bar.

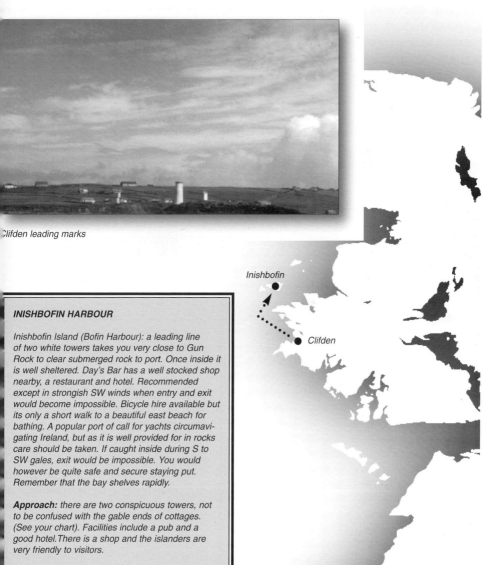

Clifden leading marks

Inishbofin

Clifden

INISHBOFIN HARBOUR

Inishbofin Island (Bofin Harbour): a leading line of two white towers takes you very close to Gun Rock to clear submerged rock to port. Once inside it is well sheltered. Day's Bar has a well stocked shop nearby, a restaurant and hotel. Recommended except in strongish SW winds when entry and exit would become impossible. Bicycle hire available but its only a short walk to a beautiful east beach for bathing. A popular port of call for yachts circumavigating Ireland, but as it is well provided for in rocks care should be taken. If caught inside during S to SW gales, exit would be impossible. You would however be quite safe and secure staying put. Remember that the bay shelves rapidly.

Approach: *there are two conspicuous towers, not to be confused with the gable ends of cottages. (See your chart). Facilities include a pub and a good hotel. There is a shop and the islanders are very friendly to visitors.*

BOFIN HARBOUR TO BLACKSOD (ELLY BAY)

Friday 26 June

(Charts 1820, 2704). 43 NM, 9 hours

A good weather forecast with a fresh southwester all day. Confession - we should have had chart 2667 and had to cover a ten mile gap between charts 1820 and 2704 on a 1:500,000 chart, rather like using a school atlas for the Ml! Fortunately we were unlikely to need a bolt-hole, and the chart showed The Bills as the only obstruction a

Inishbofin

good 38 miles to our starboard (east) Even so The Bills are an awe-inspiring group of steep-to rocks, and home to numerous sea birds as their vicinity abounds with fish. Achill and Saddle Heads were very dramatic. We saw only one boat, a purposeful-looking Fisheries Protection vessel, all day until we entered Blacksod Bay, when a local was going for an evening sail Each meeting of a yacht qualifies for log entry. Elly Bay seemed to be the recommended bay in Blacksod Bay, but there were no other boats at all and no moorings, only a smart boating club with a few dinghies and canoes on the north side. Mullet, the land enclosing Blacksod Bay, is effectively a large island, only connected to the mainland by a bridge over a canal at Belmullet, and sparsely populated. Although well-sheltered we felt rather lonely here, but didn't go ashore and had an early night.

Calls to Belmullet Radio, who in turn called the Coastguard for us, elicited that the Belmullet canal is now closed (technically it was 'open' but only for dinghies able to get under now the fixed bridge); had it been open it would have reduced tomorrow's passage to a few inland miles.

chill Head

addle Head

nishbofin Fort

> ### BLACKSOD BAY
>
> *The Irish Cruising Club and CA recommend Elly Bay, if you stay clear of the moorings. We found no moorings and feel there is nothing worth going ashore for. Sailing Club on N side.*
> *Blacksod Bay is surely worth the extra trouble and saves 4 unnecessary miles. The bridge over the canal into Blacksod Bay is now fixed. This is a large open bay about 3M wide by 9M long. There are many smaller bays, so many that you can make a choice depending on the wind. Beware that many of them shoal at their heads. Elly Bay is one of the best anchorages. Anchor outside of local boats. Facilities are about 1.5M inland. Post Office, petrol, diesel and some limited groceries.*

Blacksod - Elly Bay

Inishbofin

BLACKSOD BAY TO BROADHAVEN (Co. Mayo)

Saturday 27 June

(Charts 2704, 2703). 30NM, 5 hours 35 minutes

Erris Head

We awoke to a light nort wind which was to give u quiet seas for a change. W took an inshore passag first passing through th shallow and narrov Duvillan Sound. Keepin two white beacons on th offshore Iniskea Sout Island in line kept us clear c rocks through quite roug water. This passage is onl recommended in fine weathe and was made possible b the excellent directions i the Admiralty Sailin Directions. Continuing nort inside the Inishglora islands an Eagle Island with a white towered lighthouse, we rounde another notable headland, Erri Head, giving the extensive ove falls marked on the chart a wid berth, and turned southeast t enter Broadhaven. We anchore south of Gubaknockan jetty, an on approaching this in the dingh we were waved to come alongsid the lifeboat, it being their annua open day. It was a magnificent boa in splendid condition, the RNL MABEL WILLIAMS. Electroni charting was being enthusiasticall demonstrated, and is nov preferred to paper charts which 'sli about' under rough conditions.

A very kind Liverpudlian on the quay offered to drive us 6 miles into Belmullet, with the nearest shops and a small supermarket, and then took us to see the semi-derelict cottage he had bought with a 270 degree sea view over Blacksod Bay. He is teaching his neighbour, who never went to school, to read and write, in return for help with planning permission. This neighbour never knew his middle name, and although they found his birth certificate it was indecipherable so they were none the wiser. On the way we drove over the canal which had a clean dry bottom at low water and could be used by a dinghy at high water.

Saddle Head

RNLB MABEL WILLIAMS

Broadhaven
Blacksod -
Elly Bay

BROADHAVEN

A well placed natural harbour giving good shelter during the summer months. 5M long and 1M wide in some places. The sea breaks at the entrance in north or north west gales. It should not be entered at these times. Anchor near shore south of Ballyglass Pier and NW of lifeboat mooring to avoid light swell which causes severe rolling. No facilities, not even rubbish disposal. Could lie alongside trawler on pier. The nearest shops are at Bellmulett which has a small general store. There is a telephone.

BROADHAVEN TO KILLYBEGS

Sunday 28 June

(Charts 2703, 2767, 2702). 60 NM (on chart), 11 hours 37 minutes

This 'day of rest' was not to be as the tide and distance dictated a start just before 0500. The westerly wind steadily rose and we had a real roller-coaster with the sea building to a most uncomfortable four to five metres. I had set a waypoint off Teelin so that we

Killybegs

could, if necessary, go directly there, but I was keen to see Killybegs and we were making such could speed in Donegal Bay that we decided to continue Much of our speed was genuinely over 6kts and we ended up with single reefed main with preventer and 17 rolls in the genoa. In attempting to take in a second reef we inadvertently gybed, the preventer breaking off the river through the swivel on the main sheet block. The untethered boom, now totally out of control swung out fully to starboard. Fortunately we only had 10NM to do before turning to port into the shelter of Killybegs, a magnificent harbour, when all was quiet again, and were able to turn into the wind and tame the boom. The alternative of motoring into the wind and attempting to secure a wildly gyrating boom in order to lower the mainsail was virtually unthinkable for a man and wife crew, and emphasized the need to keep all gear in top-notch order; I was horrified subsequently to see the small diameter, about $3/16''$, of the stud that takes the full load of the main sheet.

We anchored in the place recommended in the CA Handbook (but it would be impossible to land here, the shore comprising a steep loose rock wall onto closed commercial property), when a local yachtsman out with his Hunter yacht and dog for an evening sail came close by and recommended we moved to the anchorage between the piers. There were no fishing vessel movements, and this was much more sheltered and friendly. We met Scott Bayfield (Royal Ocean Cruising Club) on PHYSALIAN, circumnavigating Ireland and horse-riding.

I took the broken block into Mooney Engineering, a superb operation. They turned down the head of an 8mm bolt, shortened it, drilled out one part of the swivel to 8mm, filed away enough plastic to accommodate a lock nut, and all for £6 including a spare nut, so it became stronger than ever. I acted as an assistant throughout, and my intelligent interest perhaps helped to achieve this moderate charge! I called at Swan Net for some lengths of 6mm rope with heat sealed ends. They charged nothing and threw in the rest of the spool of rope. Killibegs is therefore highly recommended, and provides good fish and chips too. Margo bought a Donnegal hand-loomed jumper for £30 with which she is delighted.

KILLYBEGS

Highly recommended.A major fishing and commercial port set in fine surroundings. It provides good shelter and can be entered by day or night. A superb all-weather harbour with all facilities although diesel has to be ordered and delivered by tanker. Mooney Boats have first class engineering facilities including fittings, mainly heavy. Swan Net supplies rope. Water hydrants on the quay between piers. The Harbour Master will obtain fax forecasts. Fish and chip shop. Banks with cash dispensers. Shop open Sundays.

Anchor in NW corner of harbour where there is now no significant fishing boat activity, not where recommended to anchor,where going ashore up a dumped boulder wall is not practicable; land at steps on east side of fishing pier. Good holding in mud. A mooring may be free. Yachts should not be left unattended except for very short periods. If given permission you can lie along the pier for water and stores. Beware of anchoring in Port Roshin where the holding is poor and there are uncharted rocks. There is also a danger from lost ground tackle in all anchorages.

Approach: Keep in the mid channel, leaving Rotten Island to starboard. Locate buoy off Rough Point and head for the South Cardinal buoy on the harbour shoal. When 1/2ca south of this buoy turn in towards the quays.

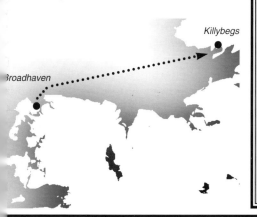

Killybegs

Broadhaven

KILLYBEGS TO TEELIN

Monday 29 June

(Chart 2702). 11 NM, 2 hours 30 minutes

At 1600 we left for the inshore passage to Teelin, passing north of the Black Rock (which is low- lying and genuinely black) and Inishduff island. Approaching Muckrow Head we encountered drift nets necessitating a long diversion before entering Teelin harbour and moored on one of Ireland's new state buoys (like the Scottish Highland & Island ones) labelled with a maximum of 15 tonnes. Unfortunately these look out to

Teelin

the open sea and would be untenable in strong south wind. They are also very low in the water, but our Baltic mooring device worked a treat, to be replaced by a heavy rope using the dinghy. Thirdly they are far from either of the two landing places, and obviously positioned by a non-sailor. PHYSALIAN came in later, and Scott went off horse riding the next day.

On Tuesday we landed on the west side of the harbour and scrambled up the hillside. At the top there appeared to be a ruin with a win-dow. On reaching this and looking through the derelict window we were horrified to find a vertical drop to the sea far below! This had once been a Coastguard lookout rockfalls leaving the ruin on the very edge of the cliff. Two miles fur ther west the cliffs get higher to reach the highest in Europe, the clif top being 600 metres above sea level. We returned to the road and walked up the hill into Teelin village where the only shop was doing a roaring trade selling crisps to teenagers who were attending an Irish language and culture school.

On Wednesday we landed on the east side, this time with bikes, cycling first to the local hamlet of Kilkar where Margo bought a pullover from a home knitware shop, then continued into Carrick. Here we found a mill that had re-established a weaving business making tweed, and watched a handloom at work. We were shown round the other rooms where the warps are prepared, with wool being fed from dozens of bobbins. They have bought machinery for spinning wool and plan to start from raw wool instead of buying this in.

Teelin moorings

Carrick is a town of inns. We sampled Guinness at one before continuing down the side of the fast-running Glen River, noted for its salmon, to the northern extremity of Teelin harbour, 2.5km inland. We had some idea of taking the path to the top of the cliffs, but soon retired, and returned to have fish and chips in Carrick, the restaurant we had been recommended proving very expensive. On a three-month cruise our budget does not run to daily haute cuisine.

TEELIN

Four yellow visitors' buoys (max 15 tonnes) have been laid but are highly exposed to the open sea to the south and unnecessarily far from the landing in about 7 metres. No facilities.

Teelin

Killybegs

Teelin harbour, sea to right

TEELIN TO ARAN ISLAND

Thursday 2 July

(Charts 2702, 1879). 3SNM, 8 hours

Aran Road looking NE Obelisk in the foreground

We left Teelin at 0730 to motor north into a headwind. Passed through The Sound inside Rathlin O'Birne island with the tide, then past Malin More Head and out to sea to round Aran Island from the west. It would have been fun to take the inshore route (and more sheltered) but we had no large scale chart (2792 is needed) and the tide would be ebbing hard as we arrived. Identification of the white with black stripe beacon on the Ballagh Rocks NE of the anchorage was most reassuring as one must go close to the west of this to avoid shallow water to the west. We found another cluster of yellow visitors buoys in Aran Road just south of the little island NW of the obelisk, nicely sheltered and well worth the trouble of fitting the outboard to go ashore. We found Aran Island disappointingly scruffy with bungalows going up haphazardly, all trying to get the best view over the inshore islands across to Burton Port. It seems that it is too easy to get planning permission in Ireland. We met our first yachts going south here, one Irish, one from Scotland. A geographical complication is that there is more than one Aran Island.

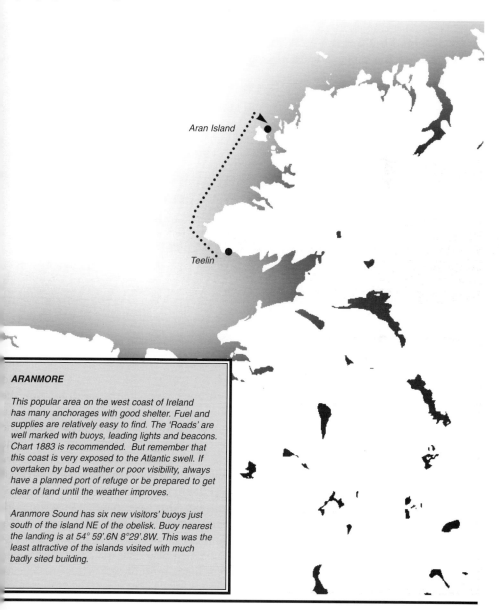

ARANMORE

This popular area on the west coast of Ireland has many anchorages with good shelter. Fuel and supplies are relatively easy to find. The 'Roads' are well marked with buoys, leading lights and beacons. Chart 1883 is recommended. But remember that this coast is very exposed to the Atlantic swell. If overtaken by bad weather or poor visibility, always have a planned port of refuge or be prepared to get clear of land until the weather improves.

Aranmore Sound has six new visitors' buoys just south of the island NE of the obelisk. Buoy nearest the landing is at 54° 59'.6N 8°29'.8W. This was the least attractive of the islands visited with much badly sited building.

ARANMORE SOUND TO TORY ISLAND TO SHEEP HAVEN

Friday 3 July

(Charts 1879, 2723, 2752). 19+15NM, 8 hours 40 total.

A grey morning but with the wind backing westward we were able to sail all day; I had been worrying about diesel as it is not so easy to get up north. The sun came out as we anchored in Camusmore Bay on Tory Island, which is quite well sheltered. A huge crane on the pier, which had been an unidentifiable but highly conspicuous

Tory Island, crane standing on pier

landmark, was being used to build an 80m extension and had already doubled the width of the pier for the benefit of ferries. This is a delightful island with proper compact villages, the main one called West Town. The island's population of 170 are mainly involved in fishing and tourism. Our gas ran out at breakfast - we had expected to be back in Calor Gas land before now - so were glad to have a hot lunch at a cafe overlooking the bay. We also bought 25 litres of diesel

ransferred from a drum on its side via a
ucket (a rather messy operation), and had
t delivered by JCB to the pier. What a great
ervice!

Sheep Haven

Ve left at 4 for a 4h20m downwind run to
heep Haven. Clearing the SE corner of
ory Island, off which there are overfalls, by
alf a mile we set a course for a point 0.5
JM north of Horn Head, which has
mpressive precipices 183m high on its east
ide, which assume a horn-like appearance
;iving the head its name. From here a southwest course took us deep into Sheep
Haven to round the Rinnaskeagh and Rinnaris promontories into Downies Bay where
here are a further set of eight new yellow buoys about a cable off Downings Pier; four
vere in use. The traditional anchorage is between the two promontories, but the
uoys are closer to life on shore.

)n Saturday we poked our nose out into the main bay, but found it very rough and
eturned to lie alongside a trawler on the pier which gives excellent shelter; since the
rish do not fish over the weekends the pier provides good weekend berths. The
orecast had said force 5/6 and 7 on exposed headlands, but it had been deceptively
heltered on the pier. Still out of gas we had a pot of tea in McNutt's Coffee House
vhere we had lunched yesterday. Another boat owner drove us into the neighbouring
own where there were four gas suppliers but none supplied propane.

he owner of an identical
Colvic called to see us and
nvited us back to his luxurious
aravan for showers (we had
athed in the cold sea but this
s not quite the same) and a
;enerous whiskey, both very
velcome and warming. Like
nany others here he came
rom Northern Ireland from
vhence he gladly escaped at
veekends. He then drove us
ound to the hotel where we
iad a very reasonable evening
neal again.

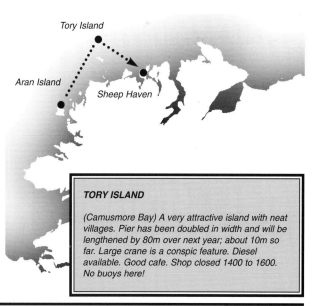

Tory Island

Aran Island

Sheep Haven

TORY ISLAND

*(Camusmore Bay) A very attractive island with neat
villages. Pier has been doubled in width and will be
lengthened by 80m over next year; about 10m so
far. Large crane is a conspic feature. Diesel
available. Good cafe. Shop closed 1400 to 1600.
No buoys here!*

SHEEP HAVEN TO PORTSALON (LOUGH SWILLY),

Monday 6 July

(Charts 2699, 2697). 25NM, 4 hours 20 minutes

Strong winds kept us in Downings Bay for three nights during which we moved to the shelter of the pier. But the 0605 forecast on Monday was for N/NW 2 to 3 becoming N 3 to 4, giving us an easy sail round to Fanad Head. Rocks and small islands extend for a mile off Glenoory and Straughan Points and were given a wide berth before turning WNW to round Fanad Head with its fine white lighthouse, then turning south into Lough Swilly to moor at Portsalon in Ballmastocker Bay where there are now six

Fanad Head Lighthouse

visitors' buoys south of the little pier. A six were briefly used as two trawlers tie up to one buoy (rated at 15 tonnes) for while. As usual these are in unnecessaril deep water and highly exposed to th north wind funnelled down the loug giving unpleasant rolling and an uncon fortable night. Lough Swilly in fac extends over 16NM further south an has a very sheltered anchorage in Fahan Creek on the east side, but on a round-Britain cruise one does not have time to make such deep excursions off the coastal route. Since we still had no gas we went ashore to a super little beach behind the pier for a hot lunch in the hotel , returning to find some charming little children (watched by their parents) had filled our inflatable with sand! This had to be laboriously washed out and we returned to BABAJI with wet bottoms!

Portsalon

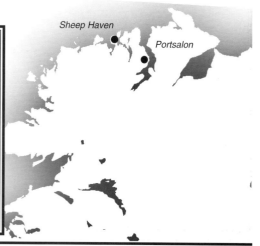

DOWNINGS (SHEEP HAVEN)

Eight buoys have been laid in an extremely exposed position, well to seaward of the pierhead, the most remote at 55°11'4N, 7°50'5W, but little used and trawlers on the jetty do not mind you lying alongside in excellent shelter. McNutt's Coffee Shop is a good cafe by the pier. Water tap and WC on pier. Shop and PO close.

PORTSALON (LOUGH SWILLY)

Six visitors' moorings exposed to swell as usual! Very arrtactive place with lovely beaches, small shop, bar and restaurant at landing. Shop and PO 1km. One buoy at 55°12'.3N, 7°37'.1W

PORTSALON TO PORTRUSH (N Ireland)

Tuesday 7 July

(Charts 2811, 2499). 43 NM, 8 hours 25 minutes

We left the mooring at 0400 for a rough passage into a northerly headwind until we turned into Inishtrahull Sound to round Malin Head. Again this early start was dictated by the need for a flood tide to carry us round Malin Head. Surprisingly with 3 knots of stream (but with the wind) this was relatively smooth - and gave us 7.5kts over the ground - and we carried the fair tide almost to Portrush. Two trawlers were guarding several miles of net but fortunately we were able to clear it to landward with

Inishtrahull (off Malin Hea

only a short diversion. The first ha yelled to us to call them on VHF, bu embarrassingly we could not under stand their accents, and pretending t understand we replied that w would keep clear. It seems unfair tha they can understand our ver English accent so well but we cann understand theirs!

Portrush is a well-enclosed harbou at the root of a peninsula formin Portrush Bay. We moored alongside pontoon which was in the process being lengthened by 30 metres to provide more space for visiting boats. Arriving at lunchtime we had a good hot meal out before having hot showers in the harbour-master's block (also available evenings in the yacht club for 20p). We found a shop that said they didn't do Calor propane, but through their open back door I spotted three red bottles in their yard. These they delivered and collected the empties. It was wonderful to have hot tea again, and we now had plenty of gas to get home.

Northern Ireland contrasted strongly with Ireland, looking very English. Portrush reminded me of Paignton in Devon. The lifeboat here has been called out three times for yachts in trouble in the last few days and one had sunk off the mouth of the River Bann with its mast showing (according to a navigation warning). This later sadly transpired to be Wallace Clark's famous WILD GOOSE that had crossed Russia from the White Sea to the Black Sea and returned through the Mediterranean. So with a possible force eight forecast we planned to stay put a day or so before crossing to Islay. Someone sent us a very long email which was only 25% retrieved after a 10 minute international GSM call. I emailed our service provider Claranet asking them to delete it but with no response yet it was still at the head of the queue so I couldn't retrieve any messages. Later I telephoned them and, trusting them with my password, got them to remove it; subsequently I found that one can access one's emails through the ISP's website and delete unwanted messages.

Malin Head

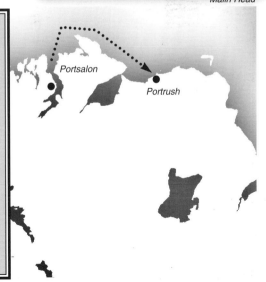

Portsalon

Portrush

PORTRUSH

Wednesday 8 July in Portrush

We had a day off for sight-seeing, taking the bus to the Giant's Causeway which w found very striking but not as vast as I had expected. We joined a large number o visitors, many foreign, taking the path. Margo was fascinated by the hexagona columns and later developed the pattern to decorate pottery. We then took the bu back to Coleraine and a train to Londonderry. From the train we saw the marina o the Bann, with the well-buoyed channel, and the river in Londonderry. A bus took u over the double-decker bridge into the city.

Path to the Giant's Causewa

We started by walking round th city wall and were startled to see security tower with its wire mesl outer shield bristling with TV cameras - in fact there were camera on towers everywhere. We spen some time in the cathedral meeting a Mr Jefferson who showed us round the museum with exhibits going back to the siege 300 years ago. Later we went round the new museum, brilliantly arranged with tableaux and audio-visual presentations explaining the history of Derry and the siege. A very realistic pair of Prentice boys are seen closing the city gates just in time. We now understand their history a bit better, but surely, I told them, this would be best forgotten? If the English had memories like this we would be marching every few days.

Bengore Head (Giant's Causeway)

Basaltic hexagonal columns on the Giant's Causeway

Portrush

PORTRUSH TO CRAIGHOUSE (Sound of Jura)

Thursday 9 July

(Charts 2798, 2724). 48NM, 10 hours

We left at 0940 after filling up with 15p per litre diesel (the cheapest we were to get), and water, both available on the pontoon. Once clear of The Skerries we set course for a waypoint 2 NM SW of Ardmore Point on Islay, 36 NM to the NW. The sea moderated as the NW wind fell from 12 to 6 knots, and became slight as we got into the lee of

Craighouse from our anchorage

Islay. We had been told that Craighouse on Jura was much better than Port Ellen onIslay; more sheltered, and with much easier access and more yachts and facilities, so we took one of the eight 15 tonne buoys there. It is some 13 NM further than Port Ellen, so we had set an intermediate waypoint at the Otter Rock some 5 NM SW of Port Ellen as a decision point. We arrived at Craighouse at 1940 and after baking a salmon we had bought from a fishing boat in Portrush (absolutely splendid served with jacket potatoes and broccoli) went ashore for a drink at the pub; this has a good restaurant but could hardly have equalled our dinner. Scottish yachts were collecting water from a hose on the quay; it is peaty and supposed to be very good.

Approaching Jura from 3 miles S of its SE tip

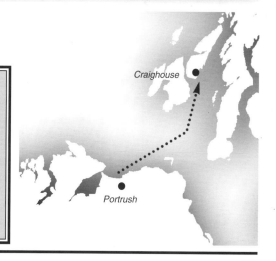

CRAIGHOUSE

This port is recommended by locals in preference to Port Ellen on Islay as an overnight port. Good shelter. Store. Bar and showers at the hotel. There are eight 15 tonne visitors' buoys with high occupancy overnight, but plenty of room to anchor (beware kelp). A handy alternative to Gigha with good shelter but subject to swell.

Facilities: Post office, shop, water, fuel, Calor Gas and Hotel.

CRAIGHOUSE TO TARBERT (West side of Jura Sound)

Friday 10 July

(Charts 2724, 2169). 10NM, 2 hours

Although I checked last night that we had to arrive at the Sound of Luing at 1045 for the start of the north-going stream, I hadn't appreciated that it was 23 miles away so we should have started much earlier. Anyway it was an atrocious day with very

Tarbert on Jura with a sea

heavy rain so I caught up with my log and email, but was unable to send it as there was no Vodafone signal in this mountain-surrounded sound. We decided to go as far as Tarbert (not the well known one but tiny Bogha Bay at 55° 58.' 0N), leaving at 1500 with only half a mile visibility but with radar giving a very clear picture of the coastline. We anchored where recommended in the

Clyde Cruising Club Sailing Directions, and wondered whether we were the first to do so this year. The entrance is partially closed by a large rock, behind which one anchors in sand, and by two submerged rocks in mid 'channel' and which one shouldn't consider entering without the plan in the CCC book. A really well sheltered bay.

The sun came out and the real beauty of the place was revealed, with a large seal taking an interest in us. We had seen our first Scottish dolphin on the way too. We later had the real highlight of our entire cruise when two otters started playing together very close to our anchorage, rubbing their necks together while their long tails floated out on the surface. Then they dived under, their tails disappearing last, not to be seen again.

Tarbert looking into Jura

Tarbert

Craighouse

75

TARBERT (JURA) TO OBAN

Saturday 11 July

(Charts 2169, 2326, 1790). 32NM, 8 hours

A perfect morning giving a beautiful start from our idyllic little bay with a smooth sea outside in the Sound of Jura, although the eddies as we approached the eastern entrance to the dreaded Gulf of Corrvreckan were quite exciting and too much for the

Oban from Kerra

autopilot to cope with. We were overtaken by two RIBs at tremendous speed that we later saw at Lochalsh. At last we were seeing numbers of yachts, once at least five.

The tide turned favourable (by planning) as we approached the Sound of Luing giving a smooth exit into the Sound of Lorne. We took a free but undoubtedly private mooring just south of Oban, and with the strong stream rowed straight to the rocky shore carrying the dinghy up to the high water mark. After walking back from the town centre to Tesco's, which housed the post office, we found that waiting mail was at the sorting office back in town and just made it by 5, after which it would have closed until Monday. Then it was back to Tesco's to shop and got a taxi to deliver us to where we had to climb over a wall and ferry bags down to the dinghy. I suppose taxis get used to unusual requests like 'just drive on until we tell you to stop'!

Corrvreckan

Oban

Tarbert

OBAN TO KERRERA TO TOBERMORY

Sunday 12 July

(Charts 2387, 2390). 24NM, 5 hours

It is notoriously difficult to find somewhere to come alongside in Oban. We first came alongside a diving vessel on the pier to go ashore for newspaper etc. Then we crossed to Kerrera marina on Kerrera island for a brief inspection, finding the main pontoon two to three abreast both sides, then left at 1230 passing up the sound to Tobermory.

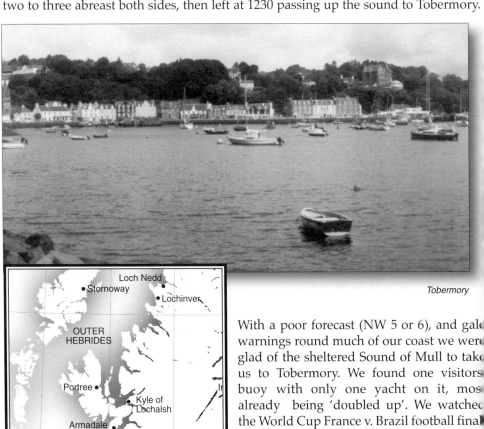

Tobermory

With a poor forecast (NW 5 or 6), and gale warnings round much of our coast we were glad of the sheltered Sound of Mull to take us to Tobermory. We found one visitors buoy with only one yacht on it, most already being 'doubled up'. We watched the World Cup France v. Brazil football final the first half in one pub while we ate beside a fire (mid-July!), then had a good walk on a lovely wooded pathway above the bay before returning to another absolutely packed pub to see the last few exciting minutes - and third goal - of play.

TOBERMORY

Monday 13 July

A squall at 0600 made the anchor of CLOUDBERRY, anchored inside us, drag, and we were glad to be on a (shared) council mooring (free!). 20/25 knots from the NW were still howling around us in beautiful Tobermory harbour but now forecast to fall to force 3 to 4 tomorrow so we visited the distillery, laundrette, chandler for a new hat, supermarket and bank (necessary by then!). The water used to mash the barley in the distillery is so peaty that we discovered they do not need to use peat as the fuel in the malting process.

Tobermory at low tide

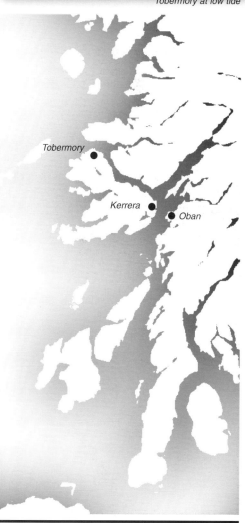

Tobermory distillery

TOBERMORY TO ARMADALE (SE Skye)

Tuesday 14 July

(Charts 2390, 2392, 2208). 34NM, 7 hours 45 minutes

This was possibly our best day so far, with sunshine, beautiful mountains around us, and light winds and sea. Left Tobermory this morning after being hailed by CA member Barry Smith on DAWN RUN who we didn't see come in last night. We had just been lent an aerosol engine starter to get the Seagull outboard going again by CLOUDBERRY (another CA member).

Eigg

A beautiful day at last - can summer really be here? - with the first fair weather cumulus we've seen for weeks and the visibility not too clear. The sea was moderate to rough, and rough around the famous Ardnamurchan Point, but smoother in the lee of Eigg. Picked up a free Highland and an Island buoy in Armadale with fantastic 180 degree panoramic view over the Sound of Sleat and into Loch Nevis opposite and the great mountains beyond

Ardnamurchan Point

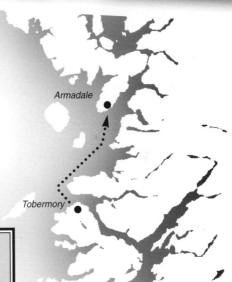

Armadale

Tobermory

TOBERMORY (MULL)

There are five free Highland and Island buoys clos-
est to the shore, generally doubled-up, and little
changed for many a year. Poor holding for anchors
and subject to squalls.

ARMADALE (SE SKYE)

Lovely anchorage with free Highland and Island
buoys. Clan Donald gardens and centre above,
restaurant by the ferry pier. Peaty water from the
hose on pier very popular with Scots. No GSM.

ARMADALE TO PORTREE

Wednesday 15 July (St Swithin)

(Charts 2208, 2209). 42NM, 7 hours 35 minutes

We had no Vodafone signal at Armadale, although a neighbour was using Cellphone so we stopped and drifted on Line Crowlin, a huge inland sea, which was glassy and dead calm. But the signal was subject to fading and after three attempts I gave up. We had left Armadale at 0600 to pass through Kyle Rhea with the last of the flood. Even so we made 12.6 knots over the ground for a while, having been through some tremendous whirlpools.

Entrance to Portree

We stopped on the main pier at Lochals to fill up with water, and then on the new pontoon off the big hotel to go shopping Bought our first haggis and a turnip to g with it, and then sailed under the bridg to Skye. When we had circumnavigate in 1993 in the opposite direction th bridge was still under construction, and we had been thrown by towers in the distance. These were bridge piles being made nearby to be floated into position later. We carried on across Line Crowlin and Caol Mor between Raasay and Scalpay into Portree where we tied up to a Highlands and Islands buoy; I went ashore with the mobile but got no glimmer of a signal even from the high ground. It seems Vodafone do not bother with the west coast leaving this to Cellphone. We celebrated my birthday with dinner in a seafood restaurant on the waterfront. Portree is a most attractive town not unlike Tobermory with attractively coloured buildings and several good restaurants, supermarket and chandlers (primarily for fishing vessels).

The bridge to Skye & the Kyle of Lochalsh

LORD OF THE ISLES leaving Armadale

KYLE OF LOCHALSH

Water and diesel from the quay. You can stay overnight on a pontoon in front of hotel. Good shops. Very quiet since the ferry was replaced by the bridge. Good GPS signal here only! '

PORTREE (SKYE)

Free Highlands and Islands buoys. Pretty town, good choice of restaurants, ship chandlery, many shops. Good view from 'The Lump'. No GSM signal.

PORTREE TO LOCHINVER

Thursday 16 July

(Charts 2209, 2210, 1794, 2501, 2504). 56NM, 10 hours 40 minutes.

There was a light following wind all day but we managed some sailing. Sketched the magnificent dome-shaped mountain Suilven (728m) from the 075°approach that took us between A'Chleit and Soyea Islands into Lochinver. A sectored light on Glas Leac a rock in the otherwise deep loch, would make entry safe by night.

Lochinver

We moored alongside the pontoon in mini-marina for £9.60 (9m); it is £18.80 fo 2 to 7 nights so a week is cheap. A nev breakwater mole gives excellent shelter t the pontoon. A German yachtsman wa spending a week here enjoying fel walking. Lochinver is a modern bus fishing port, with concrete quays and fine ice plant. Foreign trawlers go deer sea trawling, catching species we won eat and which are road-freighted t France or Spain. Possibly they dry c smoke it, as cooked our way it is tastele!

and watery (according to the ice plant operator). We had a rain shower this evening after a dull day with the odd glimmer of sun, so summer lasted a good two days. Lochinver is an attractive village built alongside the waterfront, with the large Culag Hotel behind the old pier, a church, post office, shops and a tourist office with fascinating dioramas of croft houses complete with sound effects. A pretty mountain beck enters the head of the loch, where it dries at low water, under a bridge.

Suilven (728m)

LOCHINVER

Sheltered mooring on pontoon £9.40 (9m) for one night, £18.80 2-7 nights. Harbour Master: Mr Gudgeon provides 5-day forecast. Diesel (£1.46p/l), water and free ice on quay below the ice machine. Showers in Deep Sea Mission. Supermarket, paper shop, post office. No GSM signal.

Lochinver

Portree

Lockinver new mole

LOCHINVER TO LOCH NEDD

Friday 17 July

(Charts 2504,2502). 18NM, 3 hours 50 minutes.

Leaving Lochinver we passed between Soyea Island and the mainland cliffs, then se
a NE course to round Stoerhead with its prominent white-towered lighthouse, ther
NNE to round the Point of Stoer with the famous stack, the Old Man of Stoer, and
west to round Oldnay Island and a mass of small islands to turn south to anchor ir

Loch Nedd

the well-sheltered Loch Nedd. Yachts an
rare visitors here but it's delightful, bein
surrounded by hills providing goo
shelter and a bottom of mud giving goo
holding. What more could one ask? Th
nearest land access is to a tiny boathou:

on the west side with steps and a steep path up to the road giving magnificent views over the loch and out to sea. There are no facilities but there is a very pleasant walk (with wild orchids growing among the roadside heather) from a group of cottages in Nedd to the croft village Drumbeg with restaurant, shop, church and post office.

Sunset over Loch Nedd

Loch Nedd

Lochinver

LOCH NEDD

Well sheltered loch. Anchor in 5/6m opposite the south of the island and go ashore to tiny boathouse on the west side. Path up to the road. Turn right. Telephone. Store. Post Office and reasonable restaurant at Drumbeg, 1M. Delightful walk, orchids among the heather. No GSM signal.

Old Man of Stoer

LOCH NEDD TO KINLOCHBERVIE (Loch Inchard)

Saturday 18 July

(Charts 2502, 2503). 19NM, 3 hours 40 minutes

Weighed anchor at 0900 and spent some minutes washing off thick black mud from its flutes; this has to be done with buckets of water and a deck brush before the anchor stock is brought on deck. Even so a rivulet of black water inevitably finds its way down a side deck. We left due north to clear Meall Beag and Meall Mor Islands and a mass of offshore islands, then rounded Handa Island with its great ledged cliffs

Kinlochbervie- fish shed in background

providing secure nesting for the huge numbers of birds. We saw some skua intimidating the guillemots and getting them to abandon their catch in mid air. Entered Loch Inchard and after a mile turned sharp north into the very well sheltered tiny fishing harbour in Loch Bervie; the entrance is hidden until you are right up to it, so we set a waypoint here. The 'pontoon for yachts' is now surrounded by small boats and is inaccessible, but at the weekend there is little activity and the Harbour Master was away. We arrived as preparations were being made in the huge and scrupulously clean fish shed for their annual sale in aid of the Fishermen's Mission, and returned in good time for its start. We bought excellent cakes, salmon steaks and paperbacks before having tea in the Mission. We had been here in 1992 when we had had the best fish and chips we had ever known. Instead of calling a number when the order was ready they called the boat name, and the crew would all go to the servery. We had been privileged as members of the public are not normally allowed in. After tea we climbed the hill overlooking Loch Bervie to the south and Loch Clash to the north. Loch Clash is more exposed to westerly winds but in quiet weather would provide a good anchorage, there being no room to anchor in Loch Bervie. SAMARIA (Royal Northumberland yacht club) came in with my friend Bruce Grant (Chairman of the RYA Sail Cruising Committee) on board, a great surprise. They left for Stromness overnight.

Looking into Into Loch Inchard

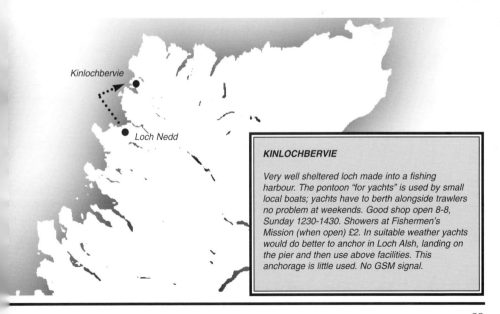

Kinlochbervie

Loch Nedd

KINLOCHBERVIE

Very well sheltered loch made into a fishing harbour. The pontoon "for yachts" is used by small local boats; yachts have to berth alongside trawlers no problem at weekends. Good shop open 8-8, Sunday 1230-1430. Showers at Fishermen's Mission (when open) £2. In suitable weather yachts would do better to anchor in Loch Alsh, landing on the pier and then use above facilities. This anchorage is little used. No GSM signal.

KINLOCHBERVIE TO STROMNESS

Sunday 19 July

(Charts 2503, 1785, 1954, 2249, 2568). 74NM, 13 hours 40 minutes

The 0535 forecast, with Michael Fish giving the small boat forecast for the week, suggested a window of opportunity so we set off at 0600 to round Cape Wrath and prepared to go into Loch Eriboll if necessary. However despite a slowly increasing east headwind we averaged 6 knots at 2000RPM to Stromness, arriving at 1940. SAMARIA was around the corner from us, and came alongside later, and the Swedes in MUCKLE FLUGGA (Muckle Flugga is Scotland's most northerly light that we'd once rounded, but its not the best known British island!) who we met on Lochinver's pontoon were already here.

Approaching Cape Wrath

Monday 20 July - Rest day

Stromness leading light

The harbour charge of £9.49 is for four nights in any Orkney harbour so we decided to take advantage of this and go up to Pierowall on Westray tomorrow and thence to Fair Isle. There was lots going on here, it being shopper's week, with kilted bagpipers marching, and the new Orkney Queen being crowned! Fuel, water and ice was available from the ice factory.

STROMNESS

Most yachts use the quay opposite the tourist information office and Stromness Hotel. Charge is £9.49 for four consecutive nights in any Orkney harbour (except North Ronaldsway St Margarets). Water and diesel (£1/gallon) on quay off the ice factory. Showers in hotel £2 (if there is a room free), at swimming pool (£1.30 including swim), and later this year in new ferry terminal building under construction. No GSM signal except on the hill above town. Harbour Master allowed me to use his fax socket.

Stromness

Cape Wrath

Kinlochbervie

Cape Wrath

STROMNESS TO PIEROWALL (Westray)

Tuesday 21 July (Chart 2249). 37NM, 8 hours.

We were woken at 0530 by the alarm for the forecast to find thick fog. Our Swedish friends in MUCKLE FLUGGA had already left, but we left at 0800 as planned with Hoy Sound like a millpond on the last of the flood which helped us up the west coast. I knew Westray Firth would have a foul tide, almost at peak as we entered, with the three tidal diamonds giving 3 knots and 5 knots well south, but I wasn't prepared for 4 knots in mid channel and with 7 knots flat-out we only made 2.5 knots over the

Approaching Stromness

ground for a while with violent eddies too much for the autohelm. We eventually and thankfully got into Rapness Sound leading to Weatherness Sound between the southeastern tip of Westray and the Holm of Faray, and suddenly had the tide with us. All this in heavy rain with visibility down to 1NM. The Orkneys are an area where tides have to be taken very seriously, there being several sounds which are virtually lethal on the full flood or ebb. Although the Admiralty Tidal Stream Atlases (which show the direction and speed of the stream at hourly intervals with respect to HW Dover) are generally excellent, the book for the Orkney and Shetland Islands just does not have enough detail, and reference must be made to tidal diamonds on large scale charts.

The North Sound was again a millpond, and we entered Pierowall Harbour at 1600 and got a warm welcome from Harbour Master Tom Rendall. Walked a mile to the store (which stocks everything from food to engine oil and clothing to clocks). The owner's daughter very kindly offered to drive us right back onto the pier.

After dinner the sun came out and it became miraculously warm while we watched Westray Creel boats (Tom's dated from 1925 and looks beautiful, but others had been sheathed in GRP) racing on an absolutely perfect evening with winds so light they eventually had to be towed home. The weather didn't last for it poured all night. There did not appear to be any change to the harboursince our visit in 1992, except for new electrical outlets and the ice plant now closed.

Westray creel boats by the slipway in Pierowall

Westray creel boats

PIEROWALL -

Harbour Master Tom Rendall very helpful, and finds boat to berth alongside. W.Cs, Water and diesel on ferry pier. Shop that sells everything 1M, and hotel renowned for sea food a little further. No GSM signal.

PIEROWALL TO FAIR ISLE

Wednesday 22 July

(Charts 2250, 1119, CA Handbook). 46NM, 7 hours 40 minutes

We left at 0640 to get the full benefit of the east-going tide which gave us 10 knots over the ground for a while. It was a moderately rough passing to the north of North Ronaldsay. We arrived at 1345 and lay alongside two Swedish yachts and in front of THE GOOD SHEPHERD (Fair Isle's ferry to Shetland). A relatively new breakwater now gives reasonable shelter to a fine concrete quay with 3.5m of water alongside, all built with EU money. We got our bikes out and cycled up to see Dave and Jane Wheeler

Fair Isle South Lighthou

who gave us a very warm welcome, an let me send an email. We had bee looking forward to meeting the Wheele again - Dave is Fair Isle's meteorologis fireman, registrar of births, marriages an deaths, internet expert and still finds tim to farm his croft, not that the registrar jo is particularly onerous with the island's population of around 50. We had showers at Bird Trust hostel, where ornithologists stay from all over the world, we walked along the top of the cliff and saw literally hundreds of puffins. They were quite unafraid of us whereas at sea they scurry away or dive out of sight! It was a sunny evening, but cold. Margo did a water colour painting.

North Haven

Thursday 23 July - in Fair Isle

A miserable morning with rain and very low cloud so our planned expedition to the island's hilltop was replaced with reading. The one shop is unfortunately closed on Thursdays. We spent the afternoon with Dave and Jane with a further email session and used Dave's huge screened PC to check the CA website, the Sailing Now site, and another new on-line sailing magazine. Jane gave us some lamb chops so we did not have to resort to baked beans. We walked up to the cliff top above harbour where the hundreds of puffins having their social hour before turning in. There were very few successfully reared young this year, the cold sea keeping their food of sand eels in deeper water further out to sea.

North Haven entrance

On our previous visit we had been to church, where virtually the entire population come to worship. There are both Church of Scotland and non-conformist churches, but to avoid dividing the congregation they alternate between the two!

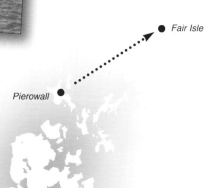
Fair Isle

Pierowall

FAIR ISLE

North Harbour has a new quay. Diesel in cans (£1/gall) and lobsters from Jimmy. Showers £2 including soap and towels at Fair Isle Lodge and bird observatory just up the hill. No GSM signal. Shop (S end of Island) open daily except Thurs and Sun 0930-1230 and Mon, Wed, Fri 1430-1630. Five day forecast from Dave Wheeler at the Met Station .

FAIR ISLE TO KIRKWALL

Friday 24 July ,

(Charts 1119, 2250, 2584). 57NM, 11 hours 40 minutes

We left the harbour at 0720, the sun coming out shortly after making us wonder whether we should have stayed another day. 15 knots of NW wind gave us a moderate to rough sea which slowly declined as we got into the lee of Orkney. We chose a rather unnecessarily complicated entry into Kirkwall, entering between Sanday and Stronsay, then south of Eday and west of Shapinsay. Although the tide was largely with us, the headwind against tide gave us a breaking sea for a while

Kirkwall - pontoon on right

A Swedish yacht CULLY that had left Fair Isle just before us arrived minutes before we did, having entered through the simpler Shapinsay Sound approach. We berthed alongside them, five or from the new pontoon at the south end of the small boat harbour.

Saturday 25 July - In Kirkwall

The Harbour Master Stewart Walker showed me his records for 1998. We were the 77th visitor this year; 28 were British including two from Shetland, 25 Norwegian, 10 Dutch, 4 Swedish (and all these today), 3 Dutch, and one each of Swiss (actually based here during the summer and regularly changing crew), Danish, American, Polish, and Belgian. We filled up with water, connected to shore power, shopped, used the laundrette, revisited St Magnus cathedral, had a short cycle ride to Scapa overlooking Scapa Flow, showered at the Sailing Club and spent the evening in the SC bar. The rostered barkeepers were a retired lighthouse keeper and his wife, with some interesting tales of the paraffin lamp days.

Sunday 26 July - In Kirkwall

We attended morning service in St Magnus cathedral with coffee afterwards. The lessons were read with real feeling by an actress which really brought them to life. Afterwards we attempted to cycle to the 'gloup' or blowhole, but with rain and a strong headwind we gave up at the Quoymurray Inn and returned with a view over the Churchill barriers. This is the second time we have been thwarted in visiting the gloup, which under suitable conditions converts an incoming wave into an impressive fountain.

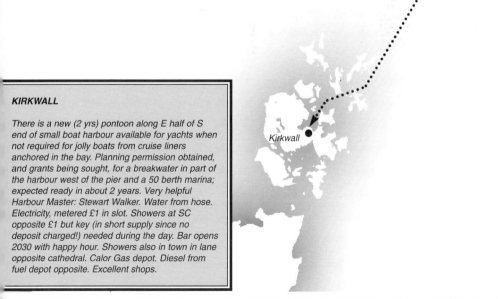

Fair Isle

KIRKWALL

There is a new (2 yrs) pontoon along E half of S end of small boat harbour available for yachts when not required for jolly boats from cruise liners anchored in the bay. Planning permission obtained, and grants being sought, for a breakwater in part of the harbour west of the pier and a 50 berth marina; expected ready in about 2 years. Very helpful Harbour Master: Stewart Walker. Water from hose. Electricity, metered £1 in slot. Showers at SC opposite £1 but key (in short supply since no deposit charged!) needed during the day. Bar opens 2030 with happy hour. Showers also in town in lane opposite cathedral. Calor Gas depot. Diesel from fuel depot opposite. Excellent shops.

Kirkwall

Monday 27 July

(Charts 2584, 2250, 1942). 47NM, 9 hours 10 minutes

Entrance to Wick

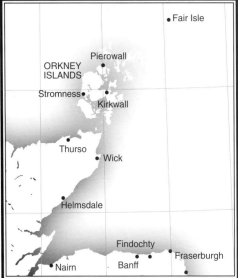

We left at 0830 with 1M visibility and
forecast of good visibility except in mist (!
but it worsened all day and we entered
Wick harbour in the thick advection fo;
they call haar. The first thing we saw wa
the harbour wall, the harbour light havin;
been set as the final waypoint. Than
goodness for radar and GPS. The wind
hadbeen favourable from the SE bu
generally too light for our planned speed
The Swedes, who left the day before us
were here waiting for the fog to clear, th
wife still knitting. All being well we will sa
to Findochty to see Margo's aunt tomorrow

Wick Harbour

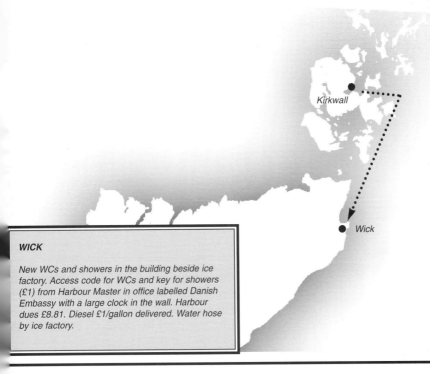

Kirkwall

Wick

WICK

New WCs and showers in the building beside ice factory. Access code for WCs and key for showers (£1) from Harbour Master in office labelled Danish Embassy with a large clock in the wall. Harbour dues £8.81. Diesel £1/gallon delivered. Water hose by ice factory.

WICK TO FINDOCHTY

Tuesday 28 July

(Charts 115, 1409). 80NM, 6 hours 45 minutes

We left at 1030 with a glassy sea and with 200m visibility. Our log records an hour of sunshine around 1300 as we passed - and saw - the oil rigs. At 1555 we heard a Nimrod talking to the Coastguard looking for a sinking yacht. The radio later reported one man drowned and one who swam ashore, the yacht drifting off the rocks 3 miles out to sea on the rising tide; we were concerned about those who thought this might be BABAJI. Our crossing of the approaches to the Moray Firth was totally without incident and we entered Findochty harbour and tied up inside the western mole. Margo's aunt Margarettie was out so we had a meal in the Mariner's Arms, and just caught her returning from a funeral involving a 12-hour return car trip.

Findochty looking out to sea

Returned to find BABAJI had taken the bottom which was much shallower than our last visit 4 years ago. Margarettie had said that dredging was overdue. Inspection showed the rippled sand bar across the harbour mouth.

Findochty marina for residents boats

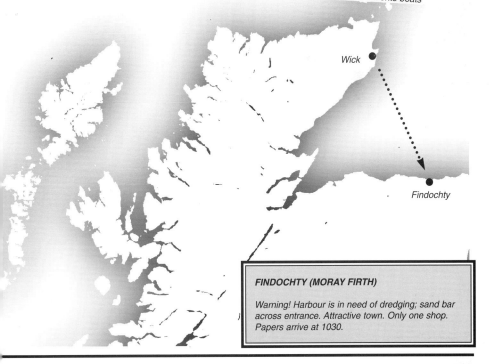

Wick

Findochty

FINDOCHTY (MORAY FIRTH)

Warning! Harbour is in need of dredging; sand bar across entrance. Attractive town. Only one shop. Papers arrive at 1030.

FINDOCHTY TO WHITEHILLS TO FRASERBURGH TO PETERHEAD

Wednesday 29 July

(Charts 222, 213, 1438). 4SNM, 8 hours 18 minutes (sailing time)

Realising that we would be aground until midday unless we left early, we made su
and left at 0400 and entered Whitehills (a new harbour to us) for a stationar
breakfast and visit to the shop. The Aberdeen paper carried the full story of th
accident; presumably the yacht ran into the rocks off Wick in fog. Conjecturally th
two men abandoned ship which then drifted off on the incoming tide; one man swa
ashore, the other who had launched the dinghy drowned. The moral is that it

Findochty harbou

generally best to stay with your ship un♦
it really shows signs of sinking, using th
time in calling for help and making plar
for abandonment if necessary.

The Times did not come in until 1030 so we continued to Fraserburgh for lunch and more shopping. The chips with the fish were so disgustingly soggy that Margo fried them and they were then jolly good! We had become connoisseurs of chips on this cruise and these ones set a new low. We left in fog and had to keep out of the way of a large Russian ship entering very nervously with a pilot. The fog cleared as we rounded Cairnbulg Point, visibility becoming good round Rattray Head where we encountered mild overfalls. The owner of Hamble Marina, who had just started his cruise, took our lines in Peterhead Marina and invited us on board for tea. We lent him the Clyde Cruising Club Orkneys Sailing Directions, for which they were bound.

Findochty marina

WHITEHILLS (MORAY FIRTH)

Good depth. Starboard hand beacons at entrance are red (with rust). Pontoon with fingers in inner harbour for resident boats.

FRASERBURGH

A busy working port; no facilities for yachts.
Three charity shops for stocking up on paperbacks.
Poor chips.

PETERHEAD

Marina increased by one pontoon since last year.
Excellent showers, etc. Security fence with a key.
£11 (9m) includes showers and electricity. Weather forecast displayed. Supermarket nearby.

PETERHEAD TO STONEHAVEN

Thursday 30 July

(Charts 213, 210, 1438). 37NM, 4 hours 30 minutes

We were lucky to have a favourable NW wind, 16-21 knots, although it was against the tide at first. We lay alongside a Swedish yacht on the north side of the outer basin. Conditions were very different from our visit in June 1993 when, with an onshore wind of only force 4, the incoming swell was so severe that we had moved violently

Stonehaven

fore and aft with the surge and would have broken fittings in no time had we not moved into the inner harbour. We had dinner at the Ship Inn where a friend of our daughter, her husband and child joined us briefly before setting off to the west coast for the weekend.

Stonehaven

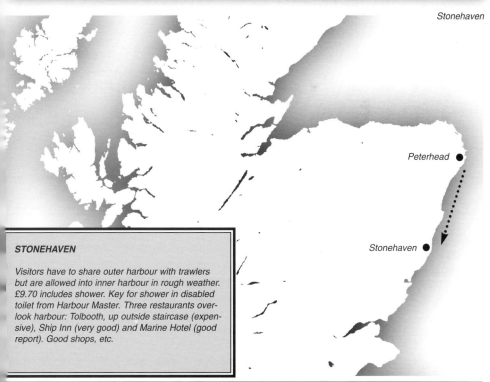

STONEHAVEN

Visitors have to share outer harbour with trawlers but are allowed into inner harbour in rough weather. £9.70 includes shower. Key for shower in disabled toilet from Harbour Master. Three restaurants over-look harbour: Tolbooth, up outside staircase (expensive), Ship Inn (very good) and Marine Hotel (good report). Good shops, etc.

105

STONEHAVEN TO TAYPORT

Friday 31 July

(Charts 210, 190, 1481). 42NM, 8 hours 20 minutes

It was a beautiful morning, so we walked up to the war memorial above the cliffs to get the magnificent coastal view and then left at 1300 just before the start of south-going tide to get the best help from this, much needed as it was virtually calm all day. We berthed in Tayport, formerly the harbour used by the ferry before the railway bridge was built across the Tay; remains of the railway line are still evident.

Tayport marina and BABAJI

Tayport is so silted with mud that it i[necessary to enter after half-tide, an[even then one has to tie up near th[entrance. The enterprising yachtsmen' syndicate now owning Tayport ha[acquired two pontoons with finger accommodating 28 members' yacht since we were here in 1993, but it had no been dredged. Yachts settle into 16 feet of soft mud at low water, so there is no bumping when you 'take the ground'. In 1993 they had built a suction dredger but found that the mud returned almost as fast as they cleared it, and had had to give up the struggle. How its former railway owners coped is a mystery. The local supermarket was still open at 2145 so we stocked up. Rain in the night.

TAYPORT

Owned by members but visitors are welcome to use vacant alongside berths. 22p/foot per night payable at the Harbour Store if not collected. Hoses for water. Public toilets available during day. Local shops and bank. Two new pontoons accomodate 28 members yachts. Depth at the entrance about 4m at HW. Dredging abandoned and yachts settle comfortably into soft mud at LW.

Stonehaven

Tayport

TAYPORT TO BERWICK-UPON-TWEED

Saturday 1 August

(Charts 1481, 190, 175, 160). 70NM, 10 hours 25 minutes

Another glorious start to the day. We left at 0800 after buying a paper, and emerging onto a glassy calm Tay. Five dolphins were gambolling in the sun. One turned over while airborne, perhaps to feel the rare sunshine on his belly. The wind appeared from the NW but only force 3. So after an hour under sail we motored for the rest of the day.

Berwick new and old bridges

Berwick is not the easiest harbour to enter, involving a convoluted although well marked course, but once in offers splendid shelter in a large basin now little used except for a few fishing boats.

We had a real holiday in Berwick - a magnificent walled town with the third largest colony of swans in UK. On arrival we found the only convenient ladder occupied, so we moored against a fisherman; he turned up so we backed into the corner where there was a barely accessible ladder. However he did ask if we would like some crabs. Next day I got the bikes out, hauling their bags on to the quayside and leaving the erected bikes against a bollard. I then went back on board to tidy up, and Margo ascended the ladder first. 'Where are the bikes?' she called down. Gone! After using them all over Europe, including Russia, they had been stolen in England! I rushed to a newsagent to

Berwick approach channel at low water

get the number for the police, and reported our loss. On returning I met our fisherman. 'Would you like some crabs now?' he said. 'Blow the crabs, someone has stolen our bikes!' I said. Without waiting for a description he went off in his car, returning shortly with the boot open and two bikes! The police car then turned up, and we pointed to our rescuing hero. 'That man!' the policeman said. 'I won't get much out of him, he is always in trouble with us over his fishing!' He was right, but we got our bikes and crabs and were very thankful.

We thoroughly enjoyed our stay, exploring the complete city walls, castle, and town hall with well-preserved prison. The guide gave a graphic account of the life of the prisoners. The prison had been left as it was after its last use, with shackles for the prisoners' feet at night still in place. These could be released from outside the cells.

Berwick - the famous swans

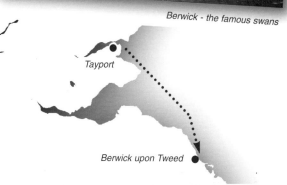

Tayport

Berwick upon Tweed

109

BERWICK-UPON-TWEED TO SEAHOUSES

Tuesday 4 August

(Charts 111, 156). 17NM, 2 hours 45 minutes

We left with 20 to 25 knots offshore wind giving 7 knots over the ground with the tide but it was gusty and uncomfortable, so we turned into Seahouses. This is a busy fishing harbour, with a small area for bilge-keeled yachts to dry out. It offers some shelter but otherwise at £7 with no facilities and only drying berths is best passed.

Watercolour by Margo Glaister - Berwick

Low water was 1958 and we took the bottom comfortably at 1740 before leaving for a good dinner in the bar of the Olde Ship Hotel (also has an expensive restaurant).

Next morning we felt BABAJI take the ground, to be rudely awoken later as she fell about 30° away from the wall. I rushed out and just managed to reach the mucky bottom of the iron ladder, attaching a warp from the centre cleat. I then disconnected the main halyard and attached it to a bollard returning to winch us back to the vertical.

BERWICK-UPON-TWEED

£3.50 per night in Tweed Dock. Tap on quay. Supermarket, Post Office and chippie near dock. Significantly less water than our visit five years ago. Apparently the river Tweed has not been in spate this winter, which normally clears the sand, but winter strorms have moved it in. Deepest water now inshore of temporary red spherical buoys and not on line with ldg. marks. A freighter from Rostock still comes regularly (fertiliser in, crushed red stone out), also cement carriers, but strictly at HW. Third largest colony of swans in the country: 450 resident but others fly in to moult and have to grow new feathers before they can fly out, so the last census counted 650. Coble-fishing for salmon off the reef in river at LW.

SEAHOUSES

£7 per night for nothing but a drying mooring! Harbour Master is Brian Graham. Assistant (Hugh Callendar) lives next door to Harbour Master's office and was most helpful. Water tap.

Berwick upon Tweed

Seahouses

ABAJI - Berwick Upon Tweed

SEAHOUSES TO BLYTH

Wed nesday 5 August

(Chart 156). 30NM, 5 hours 5 minutes

The effect of 25 knots.

The 20/25 knots gusting 40 knots NW gave a fast but uncomfortable passage under genoa and mizzen. We received a warm welcome at the Royal Northumberland YC where had arranged to meet Bruce Gran and use their telephone socke (behind the bar!). RNYC have constructed a magnificent marin with visitors, berths with water and power; have moved their Hous Yacht TYNE alongside the centra wooden pier (to improve securit and prevent further damage to he side from wind pressure); have installed three 70m pontoons with fingers to accommodate 120 members, yachts and leave 70m alongside berthing for visitors, and are refurbishing showers etc. All most impressive. We moored on a finger alongside SAMMARIA, last seen in Stromness. PIPER, a Contessa, was also here overnight en route back to Liverpool, also last seen in Stromness; David Rainborough was preparing material for *Sailing Today* magazine.

Blyth - a new pontoon in the foreground

Seahouses

Blyth

BLYTH TO HARTLEPOOL

Thursday 6 August

(Charts 152, 2567). 30 NM, 6 hours 6 minutes

Another fast passage with 25/30 knots from the west, but less gusty. We passed two lots of drift nets guarded by cobles. One was totally invisible to us, but we were escorted around it. We called the lock at Hartlepool while off the entrance and they had it open for us. Its a huge lock with a pontoon, so its very easy. The marina is vast in a very fine docklands development. We just had time before the new museum closed for a brief visit - very good.

HARTLEPOOL TO WHITBY

Friday 7 August

(Charts 2567, 134). 25NM, 4 hours 40 minutes

We locked out at 1135. The wind was calm 2kts, with mist obscuring the coast all day A motorboat charged at us as we approached his drift net and led us around, but this one was clearly visible with tiny white floats. Otherwise we saw nothing all day Entered Whitby at 1540 and tied up alongside a trawler briefly, waiting for the 160 bridge. It is always a delight to revisit Whitby, and to find no significant change which adds to its sense of history and permanence. It is a very genuine port with fishing fleet, a freighters being unloaded and the council (SBC) marina. Whitby probably boasts more fish and chip shop than any other comparable seaside resort, but has many excellent restaurants and pubs. We also counted twelve charity shops, our main source of reading matter!

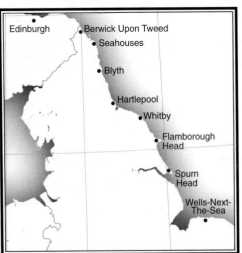

We made the obligatory ascent of the hundreds of steps to the ruins of the huge priory before dining at the Shepherd Purse, a restaurant discreetly hidden the back of a superior vegetarian food shop. One waits in a comfortable lounge until being shown to a table under ceiling filled with artefacts: an Indian canoe, ancient skis, wooden bells. Amazing.

Too good just for an overnight stop, we stayed a day, revisiting the priory and museum, and lunching at the Ship Inn which offers fish with properly fried chips, and a dinner of Steak and Ale pie at a real earthy Yorkshire pub, the Duke of York, overlooking the harbour.

Whitby outer harbour entrance

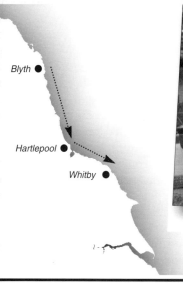

Blyth ●

Hartlepool ●

Whitby ●

Whitby from steps leading to Priory

WHITBY TO SPURN HEAD

Sunday 9 August,

(Charts 129, 121, 109, 1188). 70NM, 14 hours 15 minutes

Left marina on the last morning tide bridge opening at 0730 and foolishly dallied until 0800 to get a newspaper. A light headwind again meant motoring, but it was a better day with good visibility. It was rough off Flamborough Head and very rough with wind freshening to 16 knots off Spurn Head with little shelter in the anchorage

Leaving Whitby

inside. Anchored with "some difficulty in 3.6 knots of tide in the dark. I will now amplify 'some difficulty' as this might form a useful confessional! Aware that w might have to anchor after dark I had se a GPS waypoint in about 3 metres in th centre of the anchorage area. When w approached this we found it occupied b two moorings, one with the reserv lifeboat on it. I therefore continued nort a respectable distance from the moorings and signalled Margo to drop the anchor. The chain jammed in the hawse pipe so I dived down below to free it. However before it could hold I found we were almost on the vacant mooring buoy. But we were held fast. The anchor had clearly dragged and caught the ground tackle of the mooring. Only then did I

Spurn Head - old lighthouse in line indicates best anchoring position

notice the speed of the stream, 3.6 knots. I called the Coastguard to advise our predicament; they called the Lifeboat that had just refuelled at its jetty to our east, and it came out to see us. Their (correct) prognosis was that we would have to abandon the anchor, but Humber VHS called us and suggested we tried to get free at low water slack. At 0130 the stream stopped and although the chain was slack my attempts to slide a weighted loop of chain down it failed, clearly not getting past the shackle to the anchor shank. After an exhausting hour by which time the flood had started I admitted defeat and retired to continue the night's rest. Next morning a yacht came in and anchored about 100 metres west at the correct point. This point is on the line formed by the two old lighthouses and a yellow buoy, and well clear of the moorings!

SPURN HEAD

A popular anchorage between the two lighthouses in line and a yellow buoy, but nearer the latter, saves an hour (plus lockage etc) into Grimsby which is aptly named (sorry Grimsby!). Keep clear of the pilot launch mooring (not used).

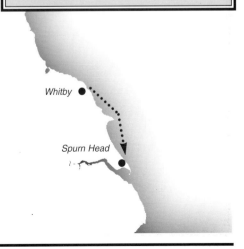

Whitby ●

Spurn Head

SPURN HEAD TO WELLS-NEXT-THE-SEA

Monday 10 August

(Charts 1188,109,107,108). 46NM, 10 hours 15 minutes

We left our anchorage at 0930 (ie we sawed through the anchor chain losing our CQ
and 10 metres of chain). The timing allowed for us to reach Wells-next-the-Sea at HW -1.
ready for entry. It was a boring day motor-sailing with visibility of 5NM obscuring th
land all day as we crossed the Wash we didn't even see the Fairway buoy we'd set as
waypoint, but we did see Wells No 1 and 2 buoys, new and clear on Rada

Pilot station at Spurn Head

We called the Harbour Master who said he would direct u
to a berth on the quayside. There was a Strong flood tid
The Harbour Master then fetched us a ladder (which w
didn't actually need as LW was during the night.

There was a very jolly holiday crowd with childre
crabbing off the quayside and doubtless resenting ou
intrusion. Reasonable fish and chips from the shop opposi
our berth. The big mill with its gantry extending over th
quay has been converted into elegant flats, with the to
floor one also using the restored gantry. Its sad to see th
loss of trade but at least the mill is preserved in good shap

Wells -Next -The -Sea

WELLS-NEXT-THE-SEA

Harbour Master Graham Walker gives a great welcome and directs you to an alongside berth (some positions dry, ladder can be loaned) if called on VHF. £12 per day but only £6 charged for overnight. Swift tide but its quite manageable at springs. Water hose. Diesel. Have to use public WCs. Inexpensive slipping service. Fish and chip shops opposite!

WELLS TO GREAT YARMOUTH

Tuesday 11 August

(Charts 108, 106, 1543, 1536). 49NM, 9 hours 30

We left the quay against a strong flood tide and with fog just made out the next buoy on the tortuous buoyed channel as we passed the last one. Had to motor round the coast just out of sight of land, but there were plenty of lobster pot floats and small boats to keep us alert with Margo on watch as I typed.

Great Yarmou

We had foolishly made Great Yarmouth (s near home) our last Post Restante address and battled against the ebb tide to get dow the coast to the entrance of the Yar and u the river to the Town Quay opposite th Post Office. Margo tied the midship cleat t a ladder and dashed over arriving with th doors closing behind her. On her return w moved up alongside the world's last stean drifter, LYDIA EVA, which acts as a pontoo and has a convenient gangway. Great Yarmouth is a town with three faces - a seaside resort on the seafront with the hoards playing miniature golf and bingo, the historical old town with part of the walls and ramparts intact, and the busy river front with freighters and oil rig support craft. We had an excellent wedding anniversary dinner at the ancient Star Hotel with our table overlooking the bascule bridge.

Town Hall Great Yarmouth

GREAT YARMOUTH

For a short stay tie up at Town Quay alongside the Town Hall and just below bascule bridge leading to the Broads and marina. Two or three yachts can tie up alongside steam drifter LYDIA EVA (open free during day) and use convenient gangway and steps over river wall. No facilities but free. Excellent restaurant in Star Hotel overlooking the quay.

Note: *Contrary to your report of 11/8/98, the Town Hall Quay is not necessarily free. We were foolish enough to tie up there a couple of weeks ago for 15 mins to wait for the bridge and were charged £10 'Port Entry Fee'. It seems totally arbitrary as we have been in and out several times during the last couple of years with and without tying up and this is the first time we have been charged, though the chap collecting the cash assured us that they collect 'whenever possible' and we did get an official receipt.* **Anthony Barber**

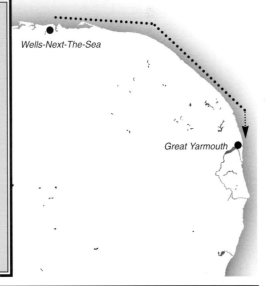

Wells-Next-The-Sea

Great Yarmouth

GREAT YARMOUTH TO WOODBRIDGE

Tuesday 11 August

(Charts 1543, 2052). 52NM, 7 hours 30 minutes

BABAJI back home in Tidemill marina, Woodbridge

Awoke to thick fog; we could not see across the river, but it cleared rapidly by 0600. Tides were just right today; we left on the last of the ebb in the river at 0600 and arrived at Woodbridge Tide Mill at high water at 1600. It is remarkable how one can extend a flood tide so long by going fast with the tide. This our last day, was our first hot one (26°C) although Woodbridge had enjoyed several hot days.

And so ends our second (and last!) circumnavigation of the UK, with the addition of Ireland this time. In 81 days away we had 22 non-sailing days, mostly through bad weather in Ireland, and stopped at 63 ports or anchorages. The total charted distance was 2449NM in 467 hours' sailing time, of which 337 were motor-sailing or motoring. It was very good to be home again, despite the amount of gardening that needed to be done, mail to handle, the CA website to work on and, ghastly thought, tax return to complete!

PRE-CRUISE PREPARATIONS

Preparation for the cruise mainly comprised getting hold of as complete chart cover as possible, and making preparations for email and website maintenance en-route; both in fact quite big tasks. Since we could shop as cheaply as at home we would need few provisions, but needed to take enough Calor propane (3x10lb bottles) to get us to Northern Ireland. We also checked our safety equipment; this is listed in Appendix I. For the crew, the crew briefing notes were updated. We had also checked sails and engine after the previous season.

Charts

One of the problems in selecting which charts to take is that the route or routes must be pre-determined; the high cost of new charts encourages one to carry the minimum portfolio necessary. The other decision is scale. We planned to use scales no smaller than 1:75,000 for coastal cruising, except for planning, when scales around 1:250,000 are preferred. And in Scotland and certain parts of Scotland we used 1:25,000. We also took BA2 which covers the entire UK and Ireland, intending - but failing - to mark our route.

When circumnavigating, a point of no return is reached, when it is as quick to continue as to return. But what if time is short or the weather horrendous? Accordingly we took charts to allow us to abort at the northernmost part of Ireland and return south through the St George's channel; this would be an accomplishment in itself. We took charts to allow us to avoid the Sound of Jura and use instead the Crinan Canal, possibly visiting the Clyde, where we had an invitation. We also took charts to allow us to abort on the west coast of Scotland and return through the Caledonian Canal. And optimistically took our Shetland folio in case time somehow permitted a return to this magnificent cruising ground. We used 207 charts (plus a few small scale charts) and carried nearly 150.

Pilots

I am a believer in prime sources, and took all the Admiralty Pilots covering the UK and Ireland. These are *Dover Straits Pilot* (NP28), *Irish Coast Pilot* (NP40, new 1997 edition), *West Coast of Scotland Pilot* (NP66), *Scotland North Coast Pilot* (NP52), and *North Sea (West) Pilot* (NP54). I was especially impressed by the new NP40 with superb aerial photographs and much information relevant only to small boats. We also took the *Irish Cruising Club South and West Coasts of Ireland Sailing Directions,* which also has aerial photographs and useful information on places to visit; all the *Clyde Cruising Club Sailing Directions*; the Forth Yacht Clubs Association's *Pilot Handbook for the East Coast of Scotland;* the Royal Northumberland Yacht Club's *Sailing Directions Humber to Rattray Head;* and of course the *Cruising Association Handbook.* The latter covered the great majority of the harbours and anchorages we used, and was essential (in the absence of the large scale charts of Dingle and Fair Isle) for the entry to Dingle and the North Harbour on Fair Isle.

Communications with Internet

After much research I bought a Toshiba 460CDX laptop with a well padded carrying case, and equipped this with a Nokia PCMIA card for GSM telephone and transferred a data modem PCMIA card for landline connection from my old Compaq laptop. I contacted many of the CA's truly coastal HLRs around the coast, asking them if they could locate a telephone socket for internet connection, this being much cheaper than GSM. I transferred the entire CA website from my PC to the laptop before leaving, and thoroughly tested both modems and the necessary software (HotMetalPro for HTML editing, WS_FTP for file transfer, and Microsoft Internet Mail and News for email).

The GSM phone plugged into a 'cigarette lighter' socket and was mounted alongside the steering position and kept on at all times. The laptop was normally put away in a locker when under way, and run on mains when available. The battery was kept charged with a Radiospares 12v/240v inverter.

We were to discover incompatibility between the Irish and UK systems which prevented the use of my modem in Ireland, so we were forced to use GSM, but otherwise all worked well and I sent daily email reports (which later formed the basis of this log) to a number of people and also to the website. I also posted reports on the majority of ports, marinas and anchorages used to the Around-the-Coast pages on the CA website. The latter are also spread throughout this book, with occasional contributions from other CA members.

Navigation Equipment

Navigation equipment comprised a Garmin 45 GPS set mounted in a bracket and coupled to the Navtex (to record position at predetermined intervals, usually hourly), the radar (where it indicates the position and/or direction of the next waypoint) and Autohelm. A link is also available to a plotter, but again this was never used. With so many charts in use, sometimes up to four a day, indexing these in the plotter's memory becomes another chore, although it could be argued that inputting waypoints into the GPS is more so. We also carried a Magellan hand-held GPS as back-up; this is switched on daily to 'catch up' with the change in position.

I carry my own design of waypoint form. The Garmin has a provision for giving the interwaypoint distance and bearing. These are recorded and invariably checked against the chart with dividers and a Portland plotter. It is salutary how frequently errors are discovered, allowing the waypoints to be corrected before they are used. I have a discipline of always using straight line courses between waypoints (except when

rounding headlands, when radar is useful to keep off by an appropriate distance) and can use many waypoints a day. I was once saved by this when a gale sprang up accompanied by fog in a complex passage through the Finnish archipelago. Once under way this method, using crosstrack error to stay on course, is easier than using a plotter, especially when chart changes are involved.

The other major equipment was radar, kept on at all times when under power and left on standby when necessary under sail; and Navtex, used to receive shipping forecasts twice daily (although we listen to the forecasts on Radio 4) when conditions are deteriorating or changing, as well as for navigation and gale warnings.

Sails and Engine

After our 1996 season our sail maker had said the mainsail should be replaced after the next season, and this we did, to set out with a brand new and very stiff sail. Following a scare when the engine kept on cutting out during a gale in the Finnish archipelago in 1997, we had fitted two primary fuel filters with individual valving so that these could be quickly interchanged in case of a fuel filter blockage. In fact we had no further cause to change over; all the rubbish in the tanks must have been filtered out in that gale! The engine had been properly winterized, and started first time when tested before launching.

RULES FOR CREW ON BABAJI

1 Harnesses clipped to jackstays must be worn when going forward under way, especially at night.

2 One hand to hold on, one to work with.

3 Men must not pee overboard; most MOBs result from this practice.

4 Be familiar with the safety equipment list, and understand it.

5 No smoking except on the foredeck or in the cockpit if the door is already closed.

6 Drinks must never be placed on the chart table.

7 Blue Ensign is hoisted at 0800 and lowered at 2000 in harbour. It is worn under way but furled after dark, when it may obscure the stern light.

8 Mainsail halyard falls are to be secured in the RYA-approved manner, and not hanked.

9 Sail covers are to be fitted after berthing, and anti-sheet slapping bungees fitted.

10 Please volunteer for about one hour's maintenance a day! (eg whipping rope ends, polishing brass, cleaning GRP and windows, applying teak oil if necessary).

SAFETY EQUIPMENT ON BABAJI

fire extinguishers - make sure you know where and what they are (CO2 and dry powder forward, Halon and AAA in wheelhouse)

Fire blanket - to the left of the galley sink

Fog Horn - forward port side of the cockpit (spare cartridge in aft locker under the main berth)

Lifesling - pushpit (Open the top, throw float overboard, circle the MOB)

Dan Buoy - pushpit (Throw overboard; it auto inflates and lights)

Tri-Buckle MOB recovery 'sail' - pushpit when under way - (demonstrate use)

MOB buttons on GPS set (see Dymo label)

Jackstays, harnesses and lines - must be used on deck at sea

Flare pack - in locker under the transverse bench seat in wheelhouse

Verey pistol - on shelf to the left and below wheel (white illuminating shells)

VHF radio - normal aerial on main mast, second aerial on mizzen. Handheld VHF and connector to use with main aerial - in wheelhouse

Emergency VHF aerial - hangs on rigging

EPIRB - starboard side of door into wheelhouse (sends out BABAJI MSTC)

Rigging cutters - in right-hand locker, starboard side, of wheelhouse

Bilge pump - in cockpit

Emergency engine bilge pump - on changeover valve in engine compartment

Engine stop - pull knob (forward of wheelhouse throttle)

Fuel cut-off - on primary fuel filters in engine compartment

Gas alarm - in hanging locker - rather pathetic whistle

INDEX